DECLUTTERING
AND
MINIMALISM

99 Minimalism Ways and Strategies to Declutter your Home, Life and Mind

TABLE OF CONTENTS

Decluttering
50 Minimalism Ways and Strategies to
Declutter your Home and Life

Declutter Your Mind
Proven Strategies And Steps On How
To Declutter Your Mind, Home and Life

Decluttering

50 Minimalism Ways and Strategies to Declutter your Home and Life

Introduction

I want to thank you and congratulate you for purchasing the book, *Decluttering: 50 Minimalism Ways and Strategies to Declutter Your Home and Life.* This book contains proven steps and strategies on how to reduce the clutter, minimize the belongings that you may have and provides a way to organize thoughts to result in a more fulfilling and simplistic lifestyle. Several barriers may prove inhibitory to minimalism, key among them, resistance to change. Change may be hard as we have become attached to routines and things. We allow our homes and minds to become storage spaces for every passing fancy and in the process, we get so busy trying to attain these objects that we end up not having time to enjoy that which we have already accumulated.

The corporations can be afforded some of the blame but truth be told they are just doing what they were created to do. That would be to make sure the products are out of their shelves and in our homes. It does not matter what trick they use to distract or misdirect as long as they achieve their objective and they do not care about your general wellbeing. Once the truth of the last statement is internalized you can start to think about how to regain your life back from the very things that have kept you prisoner within your space for a very long time. It sounds like the logical thing to do by living with less considering it will mean less to clean, less debt which means less stress. Overall that would mean more energy and money to go around. That would imply that many people are actually ready to minimalize but they usually get stumped by the next step which is where to begin. Then you end up with several individuals who are of the mindset that they can and should survive with less but they are literally trapped by everything that they have. This leads to being overwhelmed and defeated by the very idea. The journey of de-cluttering needn't be as hard as most would make it out to be.

Minimalism is the absolute opposite of consumerism whose philosophy is to entertain yourself with anything that you would desire at any time of the day and night provided you has the means to do so. That is the reason for 24-hour stores and online door to door service delivery. Societally speaking we have a glut of products and services. Anything can be attained at the click of a button and a few hours wait even if it leads to the debt of the buyer. Consumerism would have you overspend on the holidays because of the season theme and still overspend several times during the year because of sales promotions or just plain availability of the product. In your heart of hearts, you know that you do not need the latest iPhone or that antique that was allegedly availed at the curio shop because you bought three of those each year for the past three years. The voice in your head saying you need all of it has been carefully engineered to lead you to the cashier and not make you the wiser until you reach home. In order to combat consumerism, it would need a conscious effort to abstain from it and focus on how you have lived your life and how you would like to proceed going forward.

Minimalism can be approached from a philosophical point of view and we can discuss how the new approach is going to make our lives better and result in a change in the community. De-cluttering can thus, be approached in the same way that dieting is done. That means we can go right in and account for everything that we own as a person and rate it on a scale then assign a value like the way food is assigned calories. Then we can hack things off from that list according to ranking so as to 'starve' ourselves. A lot of the time though, many people feel deprived and go on a binge thereafter so they wind up right where they started. So the thing would be to change a lot of things including the coping habits in times of lack. The development of a de-cluttering mindset will mean changing the way that you make decisions concerning the valuables that you already have and the stuff that is included in everyday life. Instead of being a short-term solution, things become a long-term commitment or solution to a new way of life.

Now this book will cover 50 minimalism ways to de-clutter not just your home but also your life. So these tenets can be used in every other area surrounding the home environment and to change the way that you live life in an effective manner. The first part of the book will consider the home and various aspects around it. Other aspects to be considered in the 5 process challenge include expecting change, indulging less, cleaning out social media and managing holiday excess. Of course, the home is the primary area of concern when it comes to de-cluttering but it is not the only place that requires this school of thought. It can, however, be used as a starting point that can germinate to other areas of life. Now each area of the house presents a unique challenge. You can opt to go room by room and explore more dynamic ways to tackle each of them. You can start with the family room and debate the merits of each piece of furniture or go into the bedroom where you can purge the excess to come up with a peaceful setting. The kitchen and the garage would follow after the bedroom and closets. Each room would follow a thorough dress down to see what is needed and what is not. All of this can be jotted down in the ranking system that was previously claimed and used as a means for justifying the materials that you don't really need. Then you will be able to explore how being a minimalist would make you a better citizen on earth and help with such things as conservation. You can also look at the main impact of your consumer choices and examine the human and environmental toll on the things which you buy.

Chapter 1

Changing your mindset

Changing perspectives

The first thing to do is to reset the way you think before reducing the number of things within your environment. You have to believe that simplicity has to have some merit. You should adopt the philosophy that less is more and so the more things that you have the less value you attain or the less effective you actually are. This style of thinking makes less appear attractive regardless of the value that is assigned to the materials. It is not a good way of ranking materials you may have considering the purpose if just to reduce the overall number of things that you may have to a lesser number. This method does not assign the value to particular things so there is no way to know what you actually need and what you do not. As a rudimental way to start, it is great because it keeps purchases to a minimum and maintains things can always get accomplished with the minimum amount of resources. That is a great way to reduce the amount of clutter especially after seasons that warrant it such as Christmas and Thanksgiving. It is not going to be easy to use this mindset, it is worth it in the long run if you are successful.

Let go of things

If you have things that are in your residence that you rarely use or have as keepsakes then it would be time to let them go. You can give them away for goodwill or better yet sell them so that you do not feel they went at a complete loss. Of course, the majority of these items are from an earlier event or period of your life that emotional significance but the reality is you do not need them to keep living. They represent nostalgia of a time that may have meant a lot to you but the reality is they are holders of memories which are not always visited except occasionally. Even if they are valuable they still end up clogging physical and emotional space. The trouble is when you start having a lot of keepsakes, there is rarely a metric to know what is worth keeping and what is not. You end up keeping every last thing to remind you of specific events and soon you end up with a section of the house looking like a museum. They eventually end up holding you back as a person as they get in the way. This is not one of the popular perspectives on the matter since keepsakes are intrinsically connected to the psyche of many but the reality is letting go of things does more good over the long term.

Purchase mindfully

A lot of the time, people make purchases out of boredom or faint want rather than need. Retail therapy as it is known is an oxymoron. There is little to be gained by going on a shopping spree of things that felt good at their purchase but present a burden once they are brought back to the house.

That is what the retailers never tell you. Apparently, you need everything that they have and they are very good at convincing you that you do up to the point the transaction has been done. Before getting out your wallet or clicking on the checkout page, you should ask yourself if you are going to use that item years from now. You can use this as a strict measure, empirically if possible. If the answer happens to be no then you know what you have to do. This question should not even be considered for items that are out of your budget. Debt should not be in the same conversation. Again, that is not very popular with most of the credit card wielding population though you would be shocked at the number of people who are in debt due to things that did not give satisfaction past the first few days or even hours.

Create personal boundaries

If you happen to be one of those people often referred to as yes-people or people pleasers, then you regularly allow others to cross your personal boundaries. Your friends may gift you things a lot of place things in your care regularly for safekeeping while they are traveling for work or leisure. A lot of the time, they may be unable to reclaim their items or not want to in the first place. In this case, you become left with these items that you did not want in the first place and no idea on how to get rid of them. The other scenario is buying things with your friends or family especially during the holiday seasons for its sake. You still end up with all these on the spot purchases and gifts that if you soul searched, were absolutely unnecessary especially on your wallet. You may sound like a killjoy when you refuse to go through the entire process or worse yet cheap, but it will pay out in the end when you don't have to go through your receipts, in the end, to see what caused such a dent in your account and can actually walk around the house.

Take a second opinion

There are a number of strategies on offer to assist you to change your viewpoint and begin to notice some of the clutter that you may have missed. This approach involves taking photos of the house and asking someone else to critically consider what they may do with space or what they would have in their home. It may be a close friend or work colleague depending on how brave you are with your personal space. Not many people would be comfortable with letting others critically assess the way they have arranged their personal space because it makes them quite vulnerable and the majority of people they would entrust with such a task would not provide an objective assessment. So this is not something that everyone can do, though you would be surprised with how effective the results can be. Better yet a neighbor's child can be invited for a play date with your child and you can ask them on their opinion. They are usually brutal and surprisingly efficient sometimes.

The objective remains to see the house thereafter in a new light in terms of what can be discarded and what can be retained or rearranged.

Utilize your imagination

It sounds cliché, but you can actually use it to de-clutter objects which seem hard to remove. This is all within the theme of reorienting the way that you view your personal space. Try and ask yourself questions such as, 'If I was just buying this now, how much would I pay? Most of the time, you may find that the assigned value that you had placed on materials during a nostalgic moment do not match the actual value on paper at the present. If you find yourself undervaluing several items at this time using this method then you have a more or less statistical answer on what is needed and what is not. The next step would be to take an almost surgical approach and cut all those items away and discard or sell them without emotional attachment. Yet again, this sounds extremely unfeeling but yet effective in the end. Clutter has a psychological effect on the subconscious causing mental exhaustion and irritability so you would be helping yourself even if it does not feel like it at the time.

Count your blessings

One of the best ways to enjoy existence is to express contentment for everything that you have in your possession. Most of the time, what compels individuals to purchase and retain more and more things is greed and unhappiness with their current situation. They are always one more item they need to finish their collection or a reason to keep something that could be needed in the unforeseen future. These people are easy targets for the manufacturers when they roll out new versions of equipment, phones, and cars every year because the new items are always better than the previous versions there is nothing wrong with getting the best of something but unfortunately, that concept is relative to time. If you stop and actually assess how much has been attained, you may start to feel satisfied with what is available instead of continuously purchasing the next best thing. Gratitude allows you to experience the pleasure of your current possessions over and over again. the best thing is you do not have to keep stacking things on top of each other and you will have a much more relaxed view of shopping, resulting in a decrease in overall stress. Your finances will also thank you.

Expand your Quiet Time

The more quiet time that you get in your life, the more peace your mind gets and the more clear things get. The process of decluttering begins from the mind and then works its way to a physical manifestation. The more you find peace, the more you will find yourself naturally decluttering the rest of your life. You will also be more satisfied and less prone to hoarding or other harmful practices that are not endorsed by minimalism. Turn off the radio in the car and do not leave the television on in the background. You can start with an hour a day or even two with the cell phone turned off and locked away. Of course, this is unthinkable for those who have to be available 24/7 but yes, you can survive for two hours without knowing what is happening with your friends or the rest of the world. You will be surprised how much good it can do to tune out the noise in your life the busy nature of several web pages can create a lot of visual noise so it may also be advisable to abstaining from screen time and wearing earbuds to tune out annoying distraction noises.

Chapter 2

Actualizing your mindset

Create a sanctuary

Designate a space within your residence that you can call a respite. It needs to be clean and free of clutter. It can be anywhere in the house that you are comfortable with provided it is strategically not probable to get a lot of clutter after a specific period of time. Attics and designated closet spaces are quite popular since they are away from a lot of the activity in the house especially if you have a family. Setting up such a sanctuary in the family room is a bit selfish and also setting yourself for failure unless you live alone. This area should not be prone to cause you to stress because it can be a fallback area for work or just general self-reflection. This area cannot get junked up because it will mess with whatever you wanted to do it for in the earlier examples. Similarly, it can be used as a means to start reclaiming the rest of the house. If you have a cluttered apartment one designated area could be the beginning of a resolution that spreads to other areas of the residence. No one said that you have to de-clutter everything at once. Considering it is a lifestyle change, everything must be done according to its own time.

Organize your space

Organizing actually takes more time than the clearing of clutter though it represents an effort which would assist you to have a better and simpler life. When everything has a place and you can easily get to things when you need them it helps to relieve stress. Minimalism not only reduces the things that you have to keep track of but also lessens the amount of mental stress concerning which things are where. Decluttering allows you also to focus on more important things other than tripping on furniture and other objects that can be stacked in designated areas according to their type and significance for everyday activities. Again this is not something that you have to do in one day. You can decide to pick a small space to work on and over time, you will have organized every cabinet and drawer considering you have a finite amount of things.

Use the four box method

When you get started on the de-cluttering process, it would be advisable to put things according to four designations. The four boxes moniker is a metaphor as you probably have things which cannot fit in a box regardless of the designation. These four groups are trash, give away, keep and relocate. Every item in the house can be set according to these four designations. Waste materials may be allocated to the trash and whatever that can still be feasibly used but is not useful to the household can be given away to goodwill. There are several operating charities both locally and regionally that accept clothes, shoes and other items for the poor. The giveaway section can double up as fodder for a garage sale at subsidized prices of course.

That way, you can earn some money while going through the detoxing process. Now for the items that you have soul searched and found important, there is the option of relocation. Depending on the amount of space that you have available in the house and even storage lockers outside the residence, you can decide how much can be allocated there. The rest of the materials hold the highest tier on the chart of importance as they are probably used every day. These get to stay and are organized in such a manner they are easily accessible from a particular point.

Experimenting with numbers

This refers to the item of clothes that one wears on a periodic basis. Clothing classifies among the top reasons for clutter in most households and it is a problem experienced by both men and women who go on shopping sprees for things they will never wear after the first time they do so. Unfortunately, most of the hooks for purchase such as the sales promotions are very attractive and make many victims that end up regretting why they spent so much on apparel either because it was designer issued or unusually cheap for that time being. The experiment, in this case, would be a challenge for you to only wear 33 articles of clothing over a time of 3 months. Of course, that would mean eventual rewinding and some people feel that number is too little but you are free to adjust the rules as you would need by picking out a number that would suit you and then stick to that number over the course of three months without making a purchase under reasonable circumstances. The important thing is just to challenge oneself to live with less and then see what you can learn from such an experiment.

Manage Holiday Excess

This has become such an issue, even the corporations are issuing warning ads during the holiday season to caution consumers from overspending before work seasons especially if they have families to take care off. Everyone has gotten carried away at one time and ended up spending way beyond their means during the holiday season. Part of the reason is due to a mass collective hysteria to continuously celebrate a season of festivities. It is also because of peer pressure so you might spend because others have done so on your behalf by buying gifts for you or members of your family. In either case, the result is usually debt or overdrawn accounts by the end of the holidays. The thing is you have to come to terms with the fact holidays are expensive. From that point, you can draw up a budget that you can safely use for each holiday season like Christmas without ending up in the red. This budget is to be strictly followed with a very small margin for overspending. In the end, you will not end up with tons of now irrelevant things that you cannot use until the end of the year or that same time.

Take the 12-12-12 program

The 12-12-12 challenge follows a task of locating 12 items which can be thrown away and 12 items that can be donated and 12 items that can be returned to their proper home. This is similar to the four boxes program but there is a difference as this does not necessarily mean the entire assessment of the possessions within the house and there is no category for being retained, organized or relocated. This is especially for those who have a purchasing hobby and find themselves hoarding a lot of things. You have to select 12 items to donate, return or throw away. If you are the type to have clutter, this can be a way of solving a part of your problem. It can also be made to be fun so it can be motivational to you through making it a competition if you live with others. You can make it so that the first one to reach the goal of finding these 12 items for each designation can abstain from chores for a debated time as a bet.

Making a list

There are a lot of platforms on de-cluttering how to's which recommend the making of a list to arrange the number of things that you need and what you do not as well as those items you are in doubt concerning. This book recommends creating a list of the areas in the house to de-clutter starting with the easiest to the hardest or the other way around depending on what order would make you comfortable. Do this is in a systemic manner. Once the list is done move to the first place and de-clutter it then stops and assesses. The list could be made as easy or difficult depending on what you prefer and may easily be fit into whichever schedule that you would desire. It is a slow but sure method to move around the house and organize things into easily reachable compartments while throwing away what you do not need but it gets the job done. However, it also takes a lot of commitment to do so considering many people can start on this track and then lose momentum when they are done with two or three spaces. The danger with this is it does not become a lifestyle and one can easily slip back into their clutter.

Keep Surfaces Clean

The key to minimalism lies in the reduction of items to remain with only the basics. A bulk of unused things in an apartment can be found on top of tables or shelves where they are placed after one buys them from the store. There is no other place to keep them so they may stay there for a long period of time and you can become accustomed to them staying there which adds to the visual clutter in the residence. So it may be simplistic but logical to keep all surfaces like tables and shelves free unless they are in the kitchen for utensils and ingredients and likewise equipment. Designate a drawer as well in the kitchen for keys and papers and keep a basket on the bed for books and other things which go on the nightstand. Creating this rule will make you have to designate an area to place something bought once it is brought home. If it does not have an area to be placed, it becomes much easier to discard. In turn, this will make you as the buyer more alert to what you purchase lest it is put to waste. It is a practical and psychological motivating practice to reduce the amount of clutter and needless things within the home, thus making it neat.

Make your bed

It may seem like an unnecessary rule that was forced upon you by your parents when growing up but it actually helps with decluttering. If you conduct a survey of people that find themselves cluttering, you would most likely find they have not made their bed. This is not a symptom of the problem but a part of the original issue. If you start your day by making the bed, you will, in turn, feel more organized from the beginning. It sets the precedent for organization and tidiness. A made bed makes the room feel tidy and this goes on to other aspects of life. You will feel compelled to replicate the rest of the day in the same manner that you started the day. So this is a psychological tool which you can use to give you the motivation to clear the 'noise' from the rest of your living quarters because you will most likely feel awkward having a family room that is all over the place but have a neat bedroom.

Streamline your wardrobe

The wardrobe is the source of most clutter in a lot of homes because cloth shopping can be a just as significant addiction as any other when it comes to retail purchases. Clothing and apparel distributors have also finessed their marketing methods to entice customers with the help of promotions and sale offers. There are also designer labels that have a loyal following that would go to extreme lengths to buy the latest shoes and clothes from their various collections. Unfortunately, most end up gathering dust and adding clutter to wardrobes, eventually spreading to other parts of the home. There are various ways to address this issue considering many addicts cannot just select something they have not worn in a while and give it away or sell it. One can start by wearing a selected number of clothes per favorite collection in a month. After two months, you can select the clothes which have not been touched and then sell them and use the revenue gotten as motivation to follow through. In the end, you will have a leaner closet which can be organized and one less source of clutter in the house.

Shorten the to-do list

to do list

Source: http://www.papertraildesign.com/free-printable-to-do-list-template/

Many people have a to-do list that usually ends with errands that cause disarray to their living area. It sounds upside down but it is actually true that people with a long to-do list have higher stress levels and are more prone to clutter around the house. Most of the time creating such a long list does not necessarily end up in a productive day. Empty time should not make you nervous. On the contrary, it ought to provide time to process and go through what is needed to be done and then prioritize according to what is needed the most. From hence, it is then possible to implement everything effectively. A long to do list gives a difficult time with prioritization and execution resulting in poorly done duties which usually leaves things in disarray. This can then become a habit of taking more than one can chew and lead to a state of disorganization that you as the person have now become comfortable with. It is odd that the instrument of organization can lead to the opposite but it can happen.

Indulge less

Now, this can mean several things from alcohol to food. We have already covered shopping for clothing and apparel so the next thing would be the leisure activities that most do within their homes.

Consumption of food, especially during these times of delivery services, can easily become messy as you get what you want when you want in whichever quantity that you would like. Without a build up from cooking and dishes brought from outside the house, it can become easy to leave the dishes unattended or even leave the Styrofoam plates lying around. When it comes to alcohol, the deterioration of judgment means less coordination and more clumsiness than usual. If you are prone to taking alcohol several times during the week, you are likely to disorganize things as you would have to do things in your house while drunk. You may also end up causing spillages and damage to some of the items inadvertently especially if you live alone. Now, this would be a matter of self-discipline and regulation. If you know that you are prone to light alcoholism it could be time to take steps and try to exercise moderation as it could hold the key to some of the clutter in the house.

Plan your Meals

An organization is a big facet of de-cluttering and that would mean planning a schedule in the appropriate manner so that it yields the desired effects. If you do not have a set schedule, then you are likely to do things in a half-hazard manner around the house even when it comes to meals. Meals that are not planned end up not being proportioned in the right way. They are also not taken around the same time which means they can throw everything else into disorganization. Disorganized meal schedules can also throw off your thought process. You can save yourself the stress of figuring out what to prepare for dinner when it is already 6pm in the evening and you are starving. On Sundays, for example, you can start the habit of thinking about what you would want for every meal of the week and then go to the grocery store and get the necessary items. That way you do not have to overcompensate and then get too much which ends up lying around and now occupies space.

Clean your Car

The process of de-cluttering does not only mean the household, but also other possessions that you may own such as the car. After all, the process of minimalism is a lifestyle choice which means it should affect every part of your existence from work to home and leisure.

So take the time to remove the crumpled receipts from the glove box and the dashboard. So if you can spend more than a few minutes every-day in your car, clean up space. Take the time to wash the car thoroughly and check all the compartments for trash or things that may have been left behind. You may also stave off further incidences of clutter inside the car by putting a trash bag and wipes within the car for fast cleanups.

Fill one trash bag

As an early motivation technique for minimalism, this approach makes one try to seek out the closest thing to trash which occupies their lives and discard it. It forces you to search out things which you do not need in the long run especially considering that you have to at least fill the bag. Interestingly, many will claim they do not have trash or waste materials to throw away until they get the challenge. Somehow at the end of the exercise, they may find their bag is full which means there were things they did not need that were filling up their space needlessly. These things though may not necessarily be trash but things that are in the way like clothes that are never worn, or items that were never used

after purchase. These can then be given aw̶a̶y̶
experience can also set you on the path towards
illustrating the freeing effects the open space created will give
might just like giving these things away.

Designate a Launchpad

This is a place within the residence that should preferably be near the
door where coats, shoes, backpacks, shoes, keys and pursues would be
set so they can be found easily the next time you leave the house. If you
have a cluttered house, leaving the house can turn into one of the most
annoying activities. That is because you will spend 10 minutes looking
for the car keys and house keys. The next 10 minutes will be spent
looking for your partner's purse and various other important items that
were a must bring on your trip. By the time you live your place, you are
late and most likely irritable. You have already started the trip off on a
bad note when it could have been very avoidable. Instead of having to
search shelves, coach seats for the car keys, why not have the peace of
mind by knowing exactly where they would be if you had to leave in
haste. You would think of this area as a transition zone between the
inside and the outside just like an airlock on a spaceship.

Labeling

This sounds like it belongs in an office situation but it actually helps
with de-cluttering. Labeling is not just for file folders. You can get a
label maker and keep it handy for all areas of the house such as the
storage containers, bookshelves, and coat racks. There are several places
where a smart label would forestall huge amounts of clutter. Labeling
designates a particular place for the item because of the issued identity
to whatever it is. As such you will find yourself placing things according
to hierarchal considerations. For example, pencils and other stationary
which are marked thus will find themselves in stationary drawers in the
bedroom or the kitchen. You can also combine it with the shoebox idea
which concerns the use of plastic pencil boxes for the smaller items that

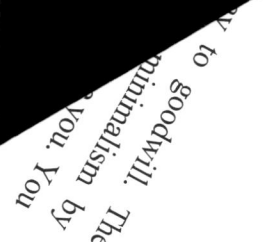

. the family room and the kitchen. They
stacks on the shelves. In this case, a label
ssible and keeps things looking neat around

y to Goodwill. The minimalism by you. You

Chapter 3

Monitoring the online experience

Place a Limit on Social Media

It may sound ridiculous but social media should also be taken into account when it comes to the minimalist lifestyle. Facebook, Twitter, and Instagram can drag you into a never -ending hole of distraction and noise if you are not careful. These are distractions that can make you susceptible to laziness and disorganization. You have probably heard the joke about setting the agendas for the day from the morning then ending up not doing a single thing by the time that evening has reached. When you finally start to get things going, you will most likely have a disorganized mind as you are trying to catch up on the schedule for the day. A cluttered mind is the first step towards a cluttered house and so you will be clumsy and leave things in disarray by the end of the day. Set a timer before engaging on social media and it should not be mental.

It requires a lot of self-discipline to keep a schedule for social media mentally. Because people tend to respond better to physical stimuli, it is much easier to extricate yourself after the alarm goes off.

Clean out the Inbox

Clutter extends to online platforms or therein can start as a practice which can spread to the real world. For example, in this case, a cluttered email inbox can sit there and beg for the attention of the user to no avail. Part of the same philosophy that motivates people who clutter in the real world motivates people who clutter online as well. You may think that you do not have time to sift through all those messages and designate importance but in the meantime, you are just letting them accumulate and you are getting defeated by the very thing that is up to you to organize. Unfortunately, this mindset can creep into the real world and you can find yourself too lazy to sort things around the house. It is distracting to have all of those old emails which may or not be important though since, you have claimed that you may need them at one time or another, you end up leaving them there to accumulate. You can remedy this by setting a rule as to the number of emails within a thread that you are ready to put up with or how long they can sit within the inbox before being eligible for being trashed. If they are important threads that could be used in the future, Gmail has a setting that allows compartmentalization of this category. So instead of spending time on social media, you can tackle the old emails and free up space.

Spend less time online shopping and on delivery services

The advance of technology over the years to include convenient to consumers is, by all means, great especially when you have to work and cannot afford that lunch break where you have to go and get the food. However, it has a flip side as it is creating a whole category of laziness and addiction to convenience. People should not have access to that much at the click of a button because it provides temptations and lets their addiction run wild. Unfortunately, these conveniences have been expanded with the advent of credit cards which allow for ridiculous levels of debt.

https://www.ppc-outsourcing.co.uk/blog/google-shopping-essential-ecommerce-success-know/

Retail addiction is spawned in this manner and the result is clutter. in order to combat this, especially if you are prone to these types of addiction, you can place restrictions on your devices for certain sites such as Amazon and E-bay or have a designated amount of time per day you allow yourself to be online. Better yet, cancel all credit cards and use cash for a period of time. That way, you can keep to a minimum the number of things that you buy using online platforms.

Set up ad blocks

In this day and age, search engines are all too aware of your preferences when it comes to holiday destinations and clothes and apparel. You may search for an item on Amazon and then continue with your usual browsing the next day only to find other offers being displayed on the side of your favorite social media site. Facebook is notorious for this. Now all that is doing is snatching your attention and leading it to the online stores so you can deliberate more and end up purchasing something right there and then. Without knowing you end up spending more time shopping than doing what you wanted to do online. The best way to deal with this is to setup comprehensive ad blockers on your browser and if possible for specific sites that seem to be quite persistent. You can install them on Google Chrome or Mozilla Firefox depending on your browser of choice.

Avoid impulse buys online

Not all clutter happens overnight from shopping unless you just won the lottery and have not yet gotten out of your small apartment. Clutter and the current consumerism have already been found to be directly related. Online platforms have been designed to hook you with the promise of the best deals available and entice you with promises of swift delivery on lesser or even no charges. Now because of the convenience that online buying presents, you are already in a comfortable environment so it may be hard to say no but there are some tips to consider if you would like to kick the habit so to speak. For one, place a 24 to 36-hour hold on any of the items that would be thinking about buying which was not something that you had specifically went to get at the store. You could find that a day later you do not need it. Most of the time when you wait before doing something on impulse it turnouts out there was no need to do it in the first place because it was a passing fancy. Being aware that you have an issue with impulse buying is also great as it will help you counter the potential temptations that come about.

Cut down on the apps

Nowadays there are apps for everything from ride sharing to delivery services. There are also a lot of shopping apps which would feed the addiction of people that have the potential to be prone to non-stop shopping. The important thing is to realize that shopping apps would hurt your effort towards de-clutter. The easier that it is to buy something, the more likely that one would go ahead and buy it. That type of convenience is not good especially if one is attempting to reduce the rate of things they buy on a regular basis which are supplementary. Though

26

that is not the only reason a phone full of applications would be counterproductive towards the cluttering goals. Media exposure and mental noise also factor to work against the desire to become free from clutter. The smartphone applications fit into this space considering they fit the bill of both media exposure as well as, mental noise. This does not necessarily mean that you cannot go near something like Angry Birds. There are some good apps which encourage budgeting or making purchases that are socially conscious. When it comes to apps though, less is definitely more. You ought to just pick what it is you require and then get out of there.

Chapter 4

Paying attention to other elements in life

Go outside more often

Now, this may seem like an odd directive. You may ask what outside has to do with the clutter that is in your life. Visualization can be a path towards inspiration. By default nature, itself is not cluttered and is organized in such a manner that everything has space to breathe and live. If you leave near the woods or in a green area, you can get to see this easily, if not then try and visit some woodlands or a zoo at the very least. The more time you spend outside, the more probable you would like what is inside of your house to be in the same state of alignment as what is outside.

The other added advantage is the time outside would make you physically healthier by default and mentally clearer. The relationship between holding on to things and the emotional, mental and physical health are intertwined. There are several million benefits that come with spending some time outside. You get to see other perspectives of life from different interactions

Reward yourself

It is important as a motivating tool to create rewards whenever you are making significant differences on the way to run your life or trying to break habits that are bad. If you are an individual that works best with reward systems then it would be best to set up weekly rewards for meeting all of the goals concerning decluttering. Therefore, it is a good idea to create a list of milestones before you decide to begin. In this case, you would be setting up what your reward is. For example, you make it so the reward for clearing a part of the house or the car is a day of relaxation or a favorite cheat meal. It can be anything beneficial provided it does not lead to more clutter. You may even choose a night out at the movies or the spa with zero interruptions. Whatever can be utilized provided it allows you to feel happy and rewarded. While typically, it is not popular to advocate for deterrence's as opposed to rewards, it would be important to understand what works best especially when one is making personal changes. In the event that you would want to penalize yourself though for not getting to the objectives though you can take that avenue though you should likewise not be too hard on yourself.

Get Some Team Help

This is not an undertaking that you have to do by yourself especially if you live alone. You can get friends who have the same problem in on the challenge. Regardless of whether you are trying to do it by yourself or part of a family, making the decluttering exercise a team effort is a motivational help. You can do this by making it friends and family day when you attempt to do the biggest decluttering job. If you are a family then things get easier because you can just assign everybody weekly clutter chooses in order to keep things in forwarding motion. If you are solo, then you can opt for a decluttering group which is made up of friends or even forums that you can find online. It would look a book club though instead of pretending to talk about books, you instead make one another to be accountable concerning the clutter that you have accumulated in the house over the past week and then make the time a social event. Having others who would assist in holding one other accountable can lead to a higher rate of success.

Hold the family to the same standards

If you happen to be part of a family or you have a family of your own it is easy to get bogged down with the problems of cluttering as many people in one space can easily turn messy. Though even in these circumstances, it is possible to hold yourself and your family to a standard that they will eventually appreciate. As such, you need to have your family on board in order to create an existence that is clutter free. It can be okay to allow clutter when it comes to individual rooms but this also should be a carefully maintained compromise as it can easily go out of hand.

You need to make sure that everyone is on the same page because your motivation is going to die down if you try and reduce when everyone else is not trying to curb their cluttering. Clutter can be compared to responding to a vacuum. The more clear spaces which can be created in a home, the more others who clutter will put things in them. If they are not on the same path then, the endeavor would be doomed to fail. So you and your spouse would have to present a united front and present it as a teaching moment to the children and they will follow.

Be in the present moment

As discussed earlier, the mental state of an individual is key to how they handle things around the house and affects the level of clutter by either increasing it when the mind is stressed or decreasing it when the mind is organized. The same applies when the mind is distracted. You are more likely to have a good mental state when you are not worried about the past or the present. Focusing on the present and taking each moment as it comes presents a certain relaxation and allows the mind to adequately process its surroundings so it is easy to organize and de-clutter without giving it a lot of energy.

Accept Kid Clutter but not from Teens

As a parent, you would understand that kids come with their level of a mess especially when they are crawling and running around. They do not have the presence of mind to consider things like organization and usually learn by bumping into things or causing a mess. That is understandable and you should clean up after them even in your decluttering program but the question is where it needs to be curbed. As soon as they start to go to school and understand the value of organization in their lives and that of the family's, they need to be brought into the de-clutter program. That would probably be from the age of eight depending on the learning curve. It is okay to have the desire to minimize the footprint of the child in the home but you have to come to terms with the fact there will be a bit of clutter every now and then. At least, when they get older they can be part of the process through chores. They can try and sabotage the effort at a younger age but in time, they will fall in line. Now you will have more people that you can use to de-clutter the house especially when you are too tired from work to do so.

Check the Expiration Dates and Clean the Medicine Cabinet

The decluttering covers every part of the house so it should not be a surprise when the medicine cabinet comes into question. A good way to de-clutter for the items would be ruling through them and checking the expiration dates for both the over the counter and the prescription date. Just a pass through the bathroom or the medicine cabinet may clear a lot of the clutter and give the chance to not replace it. The manner in which one would dispose of health and beauty cosmetics though is a factor.

It also factors as a chance for recycling though many of the products as well need to be disposed of in a careful manner in order to avoid water contamination or that of landfills. This is part of the theme for living in a manner that would befit minimalism so as to place everything in absolute balance within the home and in the environment.

Skip the Aisle for wholesale Materials

When you have a family it can be really tempting to buy things according to bulk so as to minimize costs. Now, this may contribute to the reduction of the financial burden but it might not be the best path to take in the event of a minimalistic lifestyle. In fact case studies have illustrated the amount of waste generated by buying more than one needs in bulk can exceed the savings that you may experience. It is usually tempting to want to get more for less but the question is whether one is spending less if they are buying more than they need. There is a role for bulk shopping in present-day society clearly. However, basing decisions on the fact that you can get more does not mean that you should go ahead and do it. This is true if one is trying to reduce the amount of waste within their lives because the clutter from wholesale goods does not have anywhere to go. In fact, there are some materials which can go bad easily because they are perishables. You need to take some time and do the calculations concerning what you are spending as compared to what is being wasted. You may also find that buying of smaller amounts tends to be much cheaper than you had earlier anticipated.

Think in the classic space

Everyone has personal tastes when it comes to clothing and apparel. That being said there are certain types of styles which are more oriented to minimalism than others. However, it is clear the majority of post consumers are not ready to give everything up and live in a tree. The thing that creates more clutter and stuff is the ideology of being trendy. Trends tend to change depending on the season and the preferences of the market. The more frequent you will then have to buy merchandise will translate to the unused and out of trends items that will end up cluttering the home and office or the car. Being trendy is chasing something which cannot be realized because the essence of trendiness is a market consideration that will never settle on any one thing for a long period of time. Instead of thinking in a trendy manner, you can start to think in a timeless or classic fashion. Items from this genre do not go out of style theoretically and you can be sure that you will buy much fewer items to have the same level of satisfaction.

Consistency is a Priority

There are practices that are not likely to work such as getting rid of the clutter either during one weekend or even slowly over the course of time then you deem the problem as permanently solved. Without a doubt, you are likely to build up clutter over the course of time if you do not make some changes in your life. So when it comes to de-cluttering consistency is the main thing.

You can set up a schedule for yourself. This schedule would include a number of smaller tasks done every-day or every week. You can even schedule them so that it will be big projects done at a monthly period. Now if scheduling does not happen to be the strongest point that you have as an individual then this would be the chance to do big projects at the end of every month. It is definitely time for some tough love so your effort concerning decluttering is not going to get very far if you do not make sure you secure it with the use of goals and a schedule.

Purchasing storage options

Buying stuff can sometimes be at odds with the objectives that have been set forth by minimalism and the removal of addictions which are related to consumerism. Though buying things by default is not necessarily an evil act. Every individual needs to find their comfort level with the role of retail and where it fits when it comes to comfort, budgeting, and even budgeting. The text opposes things which lead to such things as mental strain, disorganization and the unnecessary accumulation of things in a living space that was not planned for such a number of items. One instance where you could consider the value of buying this is in the creation of storage spaces that would work for your budget. Again this is for those who can afford to do so. Vertical shelving, the clearing of containers, bins and silverware organizers can assist you to start to handle the clutter. This is not to give a prescription for a home organization but the fact remains that an organized home with a space that is designated for everything does, in fact, reduce the amount of excess which would go into it. The internet is not the evilest thing created as well. For example, you can get great research on minimalism at the click of the button.

Establish a system of rituals

This is not as primitive as it sounds but it goes a long way in helping you to create a lifestyle that is directed toward the decrease of cluttering by a school of thought. Ritual, in this case, is meant to refer to routines which assist people to organize their lives and help them to make more sense. Rituals are present in almost every professional and practical career which has several steps in order to remain successful. A good example, in this case, is the military. Units are trained in various protocol and combat exercises every day in a repetitive measure so that they become rituals when they are faced in a situation that they would have to employ them. A soldier reacts due to the training that he has received to the point of it becoming a form of memory muscle. In the same way, the training caused by these rituals will allow you to form some kind of memory muscle against cluttering. You can use these practices every-day to stay on point so that minimalism ceases to become a chore and more of a habit.

Chapter 5

Implementation continued

Deal with Mail with Immediate Effect

This is quite self-explanatory though it can have a large effect on one's sensation of clutter within the home. It is very easy when you are not paying attention to let clutter add to the list of things that you would need to deal with in the house. Things can quickly get out of hand if you leave it unattended even if it is for a seemingly small amount of time. Everyone gets too much mail and a lot of it includes things that were not asked for in the first places. Worse yet others are like spam in that you probably never intend to open them. It is easy to let that type of material grow into a pile which apparently does not seem to go away. On the other hand, like many things that have been considered within the text, the larger that it becomes as a problem, the more overwhelming that it is going to be. This also means that are less likely to address the problem. There are particular steps that can take in order to reduce the amount of junk mail sent to you though. Though for the most part, the main thing would just be to stay on top of the flow of mail and make sure that you are shredding the mail that is unwanted.

The Memory Box

This is a box where you can apparently put things that have sentimental value to you that you do not have plans of getting rid of. They may include such things as jewelry, mementos from high school, letters and even dried roses from the high school prom if you have them. These are what would be considered for a memory box that would otherwise be lying around in an undesignated box adding clutter to the apartment. The problem is that for the majority, the memory box in itself has become the memory basement so to speak or the storage unit or even an entire home. This might sound insensitive but no one needs an entire basement or huge storage locker for keepsakes let alone a whole house. There needs to be a line drawn which outlines the limit for things that can be used as keepsakes. When it comes to this, less is more. When you have lesser, then you can take out the memory box and have some nostalgia. When there is too many, there is not exactly a moment with any of these.

Identify Clutter Creeping

The activity of minimalism as stated earlier is a lifestyle decision which means it is a continuous process that has to be engaged so as to keep it in check or else it will gradually overwhelm you. In the business world, when a project creep which is small turns out to be large, it is because along the way people continued to add small things that were one more addition to the entire thing. By the time that it was done, the one day project was now something that was worth a whole year. Clutter becomes the same way if it is ignored which is the same thing as investing in it. It can build from a small level quite quickly. You can start it by leaving your keys on the table. The next day, the car keys may have an additional coffee cup which is full.

By the third day, you might find the kitchen counter has all of the things from the bed and the family room. It is not at an overwhelming level and cannot be cleaned in one sitting. It would at that time probably also have stains. The problem with clutter creep is it is infectious if you do not leave alone. When you leave a cup unattended or a dish unwashed, the pile on can be quite tremendous from other members of the household and within a very short time, things can get out of hand. In so doing, you should adopt the philosophy of clean as you go.

Use the one for one match rule

This is a good tact for keeping clutter at bay especially when attempting it for the first time. That would mean when something comes into the home, then another comparable thing would have to leave the residence via sale, being giving away or trash. Now that would maintain a constant state of homeostasis or balance within the residence. You can think of it as the circle of life when one thing comes and another goes. If you cannot live with the new dress on sale, it will mean that you have to donate some of the existing ones. It is not a hard rule to comprehend but it is especially hard to follow through with for most people. Usually, when one commits to this rule with fervor the result is a change in the way they perceive sales items. Before promotions were very enticing and you would think you cannot live without a particular item but the prospect of parting with something in the house of the same caliber will put a lot of discipline in you.

The Oprah Winfrey Closet Hanger Experiment

https://www.closetworks.com/closet-blog_tips-to-clear-clutter.shtml

Though the idea at first did not start with Oprah, she was the first person to give it popularity. The task involves identifying wardrobe pieces that would be cleared out and hand all of the clothes with the hangers facing the opposite direction. After wearing something, you can then return it to the closet where the hanger faces the correct direction. After a period of six months, you will probably have a picture of the clothes that can be discarded without your fuss or noticing too much. They will be the clothes that are still in the opposite direction. The great thing with this task is that it puts the answer right in front of you as opposed to someone that knows you coming up and saying you do not wear this or that and have not since you bought them or for a long period of time. There is no way of being defensive so you are left with the option or removing them from your space.

One year rule

This is one of the most common pieces of advice for those who want to try minimalism as a lifestyle or at the least do a purge to manage the number of items they keep at their residence at any one time. The rule is such that if you have not used an item or worn a piece of clothing that is in the house for a period of one year or more then it would be time to let it go. There are some obvious exceptions to the room of course like the heirlooms and wedding gowns, but it is quite an effective way to seek out what is needed and what has been in use and what is not. The hard part of the rule, of course, is not going through the items and seeking out what has not been used but it will be the mental and emotional discipline of following through with the decision once the items have been discarded. In fact, a lot of the tips provided in this book outline this as the main problem though you can try and tackle the issue by making it a family activity or competition so as to loosen the tension and attachment.

Conclusion

The process of tidying up or decluttering has been around for some time now in many forms. Some know it as detoxification while others refer to it as unplugging from the rat race. The basics of the concept though have alluded to the opposite of consumerism. Consumerism is the enemy in the way that it has been crafted by corporations for decades to manipulate the population into buying the products en-mass. Retail outlets have capitalized on the enthusiasm and consumption enthusiasm of the masses by creating sales promotions designed to attract the attention of most by slicing prices a percentage. There is even a designated period during the month of November just after the Thanksgiving holiday when most retail outlets and manufacturers slash the sale prices of their products by half. There are people who camp outside the outlets for days for just the opportunity to get the items at such prices. That is how addicted to things the society has become. Unfortunately, technology has increased the problem exponentially through the online platforms that have developed delivery services and an increased number of shopping and ordering apps that have become available. All of these developments bring the potential for service at the doorstep of the market further making it harder for clients to resist the temptation of buying things uncontrollably.

There are literally no stops on customers buying things that they do not need as they are not accountable to anyone but themselves and that is quite dangerous. Similarly, the financial arrangements of the retailers and the banking institutions allow for fluid processing of purchases which does not assist the situation one bit. Now anyone with legal citizenship can accrue a level of debt getting things they will not use at any one time simply because they had a visa card, a computer, and internet. This is the unfortunate situation that is currently haunting the population and leading to large instances of hoarding and cluttering. This is what the text is aiming to curb through a series of tips that direct you as to how to practice minimalism not only in the house but also in various aspects of your life. The tips are divided into five chapters which concentrate on changing your perspective, implementing the decisions, cleaning up social media and paying attention to other elements in the life of an individual.

The first part of the book concentrates on the changing of the mental perspective of the person cluttering so they can, in turn, change the manner in which they operate around the house. these tools which include getting quiet time, changing perspectives and taking a second are meant to alter the way that you would originally look at the home and this can be used in the implementation of a new living arrangement where things are categorized as to what is needed and what is just taking up space. The premise behind changing the way you see things is to have it become a new school of thought. There is no way that you can implement the decluttering process within the house in a period of days, weeks or even a month and then the problem would be solved. The cluttering process begins in the mind so the way that you think has to change before it effectively becomes a practice. The second chapter is about the implementation process. These are tools that you can use every-day to minimize one aspect of clutter within the home or the entire cluttering process. For example, cleaning out the car and surfaces are just a part of the cluttering that is in households. There are other approaches such as the four-box approach, labeling, and making of a list which is addressed to the entire cluttering situation.

These are engineered to help you execute the process of minimalism according to the scenarios that you would most likely identify with in everyday life. For example, keeping surfaces clean and making the bed has been a recurring theme in the house because as a tradition that was taught to children from the parents, it was made to seem like a ritual meant for hygiene rather than clutter. It would seem that these actions set the precedent within the home for clutter to be kept at bay. A lot of these tools turn out to be psychological as they prepare the mind for the day ahead. Starting off with a made bed will tend to make you neater throughout the course of the day because people follow trends instinctually. What can be garnered from the implementation phase that carries on in the fifth chapter of the book is the assessment methods usually allow the individual to seek out which is clutter and what is not in their living arrangements. Unfortunately, that is where it stops as the methods claim that the person still has to have the mental and emotional strength to let go of their possessions. Take for example the Oprah Hangar experiment; even when the individual successfully identifies the clothes that have not been worn and would be prime candidates for disposal, they still have to dispose of these clothes by themselves with no aid.

The next chapter deals with reduction of the social media presence and organization of the computer folders because we now spend a lot of time online. This may then become a factor that influences other parts of our lives, hence the need to correct this aspect as well. Finally, the fourth chapter concerns the abstract considerations of minimalism which relate to the way the rest of our lives affect the process. As such, taking time outside of the house, holding the family to the same standards and being in the present moment are all connected as ways to reduce mental exhaustion and provide the appropriate pre-settings for the reduction of clutter. Basically setting the mind right is the best way of dealing with disorganization in the home and in other aspects of life.

Finally, if you enjoyed this book, then I'd like to ask you for a favor, would you be kind enough to leave a review for this book on Amazon? It'd be greatly appreciated!

Thank you and good luck!

Declutter Your Mind

Proven Strategies And Steps On How To Declutter Your Mind, Home and Life

William J. Scott

Introduction

I want to thank you for choosing this book. Do you want to lead a stress-free and happy life? Do you want to declutter your life, but you don't know where to start? Do you want to make time for things that matter, but can't seem to find any time? Do you want to reorganize your life to accommodate things that you love? If your answer is yes to all these questions, then this is the perfect book for you.

Minimalism and decluttering are about allowing what you love in your life. You do not have to focus on what is trendy or popular. Trying to fit into the ideal lifestyle, and showing off what they have, does not mean they are happy.

Minimalists have found that less materialistic thoughts are gaining them more in life. As you journey through sections one and two, consider the ultimate question - what do you value in life? By the end, you will see that what you have emphasized on is not what you hold dearest in your heart; rather, it will be the people, family and happiness that you learn to value above material items.

The primary principle of minimalism is quite simple - hold onto the things you love and let go of everything else. It is as simple as that. Once you can differentiate between the things that you hold dear and everything else, you can focus on things that you want. You need to understand that all the resources we have at our disposal are all finite. When you have finite resources, you need to make decisions regarding the ways in which you can use such resources. There are infinite ways in which you can use these resources like time, energy, money, focus and so on. The way you decide to use these resources will define your life.

Minimalism will help you make a list of priorities, and decluttering will help you get rid of all the unnecessary clutter in your life. Once you do these two things, you can lead a happier, successful and stress-free life.

Your journey is not going to be quick. It is not an overnight transition, but one that will take time. You actively have to change how you think before you can completely adopt minimalism. Begin with small steps, take a few setbacks and learn to discover what matters. In the end, you are going to find what has been missing all along from your life, which is true happiness, contentment, and lifelong friends.

In this book, you will learn about minimalism, the signs of minimalism, the steps to embrace the minimalist lifestyle, and the benefits of minimalism. Apart from this, you will also learn about decluttering, changing your mindset steps to declutter your home, and tips to simplify your life. The steps and the tips given in this book are easy to understand and simple to follow. Start with one aspect of your life, apply the principles of minimalism to it and, once you do this, you can move on to the next one. Remember that you are in it for the long haul. Minimalism is not a sprint and it is a marathon. You will need to be patient and consistent in your efforts.

If you are ready to learn more about minimalism and decluttering, then let us start without further ado.

Chapter One

The Minimalist Mindset

What is minimalism all about? What are the primary values it prescribes? What does it mean to follow a minimalist lifestyle? You will learn the answers to these questions, and plenty of other things about minimalism, as you progress through this book. The information that you learn might even surprise you.

Minimalism is a term that is gaining popularity in recent times. There are different artistic styles like Hygge and the Japanese art of minimalism. Each of these styles has their own set of rules that will help you lead a happier life; however, what is the basic definition of minimalism? What does the phrase "minimalist mindset" mean?

Minimalism is a word that's borrowed from the art world and it refers to a trend in painting and sculpture that existed during the 1950s. You might wonder why the definition of minimalism matters when the topic that we are talking about is decluttering your life. The primary principle that backs the artistic movement was to create art that is simple and offers something of value to the viewers. Simplicity is the key to minimalism.

When you think about it, minimalism has the same meaning as does with respect to art as it does with decluttering your life. You need to attempt to find some simplicity in your life, while making sure that you have all the things that matter to you. To get a better understanding of the concept of minimalism, you need to examine all the myths that surround this topic.

Myths about Minimalism

Usually, people seem to think that minimalism means that you cannot own anything except those things that you can fit in a backpack. It is a general belief that minimalism is a weird movement; it is unconventional and is befitting of cults. Here are some of the popular misconceptions about minimalism:

- You don't have to live like a hippie, and you certainly needn't sell your home and walk the Earth or resort to camping all the time.

- The possessions you own don't have to fit in a backpack. It doesn't mean that you need to give up everything you own.

- Minimalism is essentially a philosophy that will help declutter your physical, mental and emotional aspects of life.

- You don't have to join a cult, counterculture or commune to become a minimalist.

- Minimalism is about being comfortable with less.

Minimalist Mindset

The minimalist mindset is all about:

- Reducing the time that you spend on certain aspects of your life and, instead, divert all your time and energy towards things that are important to you in life.

- It is about foregoing the trappings of the superficial world, a world that's obsessed with materialistic possessions. Minimalism is about identifying the things that mean something to you.

- The minimalist mindset will allow you to value quality over quantity. This rule applies to materialistic possessions as well as the people you surround yourself with.

You will be able to lead a higher quality of life. For instance, if you lead a busy life, then make sure that you make a list of three tasks that are extremely important to you and you complete those tasks daily. It might seem difficult to make a to-do list while talking about minimalism; however, take a moment and think about it. Minimalism is all about decluttering and it helps you to make time for the things that are important. If you can prioritize three important tasks per day and work on them, then you will effectively be able to choose quality over quantity so, at the end of the day, you will be able to do things that lend quality to your life. If you wish to make a better life for yourself, then you need to consider the things that are important to you. Do you want to spend all your time cleaning and decluttering things that you don't use, or do you want to spend your time doing things that do matter?

The Minimalist Philosophy

Minimalists tend to share a couple of common traits. You don't have to adopt all the points mentioned below, but do consider what they imply and what you want from your life.

- A minimalist doesn't buy things that they don't need or things that they don't use.

- Minimalists like experiences over materialistic and superficial things.

- They are diligent about who and what they allow in their life and avoid all sorts of clutter.

- Time is a priority over physical things and shopping.

- As a minimalist, you will only have the things that you value, and it means that you don't have to spend all your time decluttering.

- Your mindset changes from giving priority to material items to the realization that happiness comes from within.

- You no longer compare yourself to others and their possessions. It will not only help you mentally, but it is good for your financial health as well. You will not want to hold on to things unnecessarily.

- Minimalists don't have the fear of never having what a person needs. Instead, they will avoid purchasing something until they need it.

- Organization isn't the key to minimalism; it is about believing that "less can be more."

You probably have a couple of these traits, or you need to think of a way in which you can adopt these traits to discover happiness. Once you strive to reduce your life to what matters most, one fine day you will realize that you are happy and have achieved the minimalist goal.

Image Courtesy: Pixabay

It is Not a Radical Lifestyle

In this world of capitalism, minimalism might seem like a radical lifestyle; however, it isn't. If you think you are one of those who think that they can never be a minimalist, then you need to take a moment to reconsider this thought. Minimalism isn't a radical lifestyle and you don't have to be a radical person to follow minimalism. In fact, a minimalistic lifestyle isn't all that different from the one that you live. To become a minimalist, you don't have to keep a mental count of the things that you own, and you don't need to get rid of all your possessions; however, there are a couple of things that differentiate a minimalistic lifestyle from the others.

Do You Believe in Excess?

The first point of differentiation of a minimalist lifestyle from other lifestyles is that minimalism doesn't believe in excess. It means that you don't have to hold on to the things that you don't use frequently. You need to only keep those things that add some value to your life and you frequently use. It means that you need to get rid of all those "just in case" items that you own. There is no fixed definition of the word 'excess' and it is pretty subjective.

Image Courtesy: Pixabay

For instance, if you visualize yourself as a globetrotting writer, then you can considerably cut down on the things that you own but, if you are happy with where you live, and you don't plan to travel excessively, then you don't have to make some changes. If you ever change your mind, then you can make the changes accordingly. The needs of a globetrotting writer will certainly be different from that of a hedge-fund manager working on Wall Street. What might seem like a necessity to one might not be the same for someone else.

Do You Ever Question Your Possessions?

Do you ever question your possessions? A minimalist tends to question his or her possessions rather frequently. There are a couple of simple questions that you can ask yourself to gauge the necessity of your possessions. Do I need this? When was the last time I used this thing? What will happen if I discard this? Does someone else need this more than I do? The beliefs of minimalism are quite simple, and they depend on the answers to these questions. A minimalist is always in a conscious state of paring down and it does make them feel good. Minimalism is not a destination and is an ongoing journey.

What Lends Meaning to Your Life?

A minimalist understands that it is important to not give any meaning to their possessions. A minimalist understands that all the things they own are pretty much replaceable. It is not a radical lifestyle, but it is a tool that you can use to remove all the unnecessary things from your life. If you want to live a meaningful life, then you need to strip away all that's excess from your life. When you do this, you can finally focus on the things that matter to you like relationships, health, your passion, growth and contribution.

What about you? Do you think you can strip away all that's superficial from your life, and focus on the important things in life? Ask yourself these simple questions and you can decide whether minimalism is meant for you or not.

Chapter Two

Signs of a Minimalist

In this section, you will learn about the different signs that a minimalist usually exhibits.

A minimalist always likes to have some order in all aspects of their life. Being organized is one of the important traits of a minimalist; however, it doesn't matter how organized you are if you don't follow the concepts of minimalism. They like to live their life in an orderly manner or, at least, they strive to do so. Do you like to make to-do lists, shopping lists, grocery lists or even guest lists? Does it make you feel good when you can see all your ideas and plans mapped out in front of you? Does this make you feel empowered? If you need to tackle a difficult task, does it help when you can make a plan of action to tackle the same? Mess and disorder tend to turn you into a procrastinator (dramatic gasp)! You always like to look put-together and like to put your best foot forward, but it doesn't mean that you dress to the nines every time you step out of your house. Your wardrobe usually consists of all those items of clothing that express your personality. A pair of jeans that look flattering on you, a well-tailored jacket, a pair of court shoes, a classic handbag and a couple of other basic items are all that you need to dress. Not just that, you tend to value quality over quantity. You aren't too keen on seasonal trends and, instead, you like to have timeless pieces in your wardrobe. For a minimalist, their wardrobe is more of an investment and not a fad.

It doesn't mean that you don't like to appreciate the finer things in life. Like mentioned earlier, a minimalist always values quality over quantity. A lesser substitute cannot give you the same satisfaction as a high-quality product. For instance, you tend to prefer fine quality and craftsmanship to cheaper knockoffs. You will probably choose to spend $300 on a pair of Italian leather shoes that will last you a while, instead of a $50 looks-pretty-much-the-same pair.

You absolutely detest wastage in any form. You don't like to waste things. It can be anything from your favorite lip balm to the tissues that you use in the kitchen. You cannot stand the thought of wastage.

The two things that hold a greater appeal to you are cleanliness and functionality. Instead of opting for decorative and meaningless décor, you tend to drift towards textures, neutral shades, subtle colors and clean lines. If something doesn't seem to offer any functionality, then you tend to avoid it at all costs. You value space more than anything else when it comes to your home. You will probably avoid all sorts of furniture and fixtures that will take up your space and instead like to opt for things that will make your home seem spacious and airy. The way you decorate your living space is merely an extension of your personality.

Image Courtesy: Pixabay

When it comes to managing your finances, you don't have to be a miser; however, it doesn't imply that you believe in living life king-size. You can spend money on things that you love, will use and will last you for long. It doesn't necessarily apply to possessions. In fact, if you like to travel and enjoy it, then maybe you can plan your finances in such a manner that you can accommodate your love for travel. It doesn't make any sense to save up for an exotic vacation and then spend all that money on inconsequential purchases.

A minimalist detests clutter in all forms. Do you hate clutter and you don't deal well with it? Do you like the idea of simplifying your life? Do you tend to reassess all your possessions continuously? If your answer is yes, then you are a minimalist. Your dislike for clutter extends to the people in your life and not just the possessions. You like the idea of quality over quantity.

If you exhibit any of the traits that are discussed in this chapter, then you are a minimalist at heart, but it doesn't necessarily mean that you live a minimalist lifestyle. So, once you identify that minimalism is the right fit for you, the next step is to start incorporating the philosophies of minimalism into your life.

Chapter Three

Types of Minimalists

The word minimalism has various connotations in the modern world that we live in. Not only does minimalism seem to mean different things for different people, but it is also difficult to understand whether everyone understands it in the same manner or not. The word minimalism is tossed around quite carelessly these days and people seem to use it in different ways. Minimalism is quite an abstract concept and there are different ways in which you can follow it. In this section, you will learn about the different types of minimalists, but there is one concept that binds all types of minimalists and it is the idea of "less is more."

Image Courtesy: Pixabay

Aesthetic Minimalist

The main focus of an aesthetic minimalist is optics. It doesn't necessarily mean that they own less. They might or might not even own less, but they certainly like to have only a few things on display. White is the one color that aesthetic minimalists are drawn to, and they try to incorporate this in the aesthetics of their surroundings. In fact, it is quite easy to spot an aesthetic minimalist. They always opt for clean lines, open spaces and neutral colors. So, if you walk into someone's house and notice bare walls and bare countertops, then it is quite likely that you walked into the house of a minimalist.

Essential Minimalist

An essential minimalist is someone who likes to stick to the bare essentials and nothing more. They constantly keep updating their list of essential items and keep checking on what are the things that they can live with or without. Essential minimalists like to use less and even own less. They are constantly paring down their belongings. In fact, this is the defining trait of all essential minimalists. Going back to the basics seems to be their ideology. Quality and quantity matter to them and the one that they absolutely loathe is wastage. They detest wastage in all forms. They don't horde things and will discard old things to make room for new acquisitions. They try to do all this within their means and will not like to make any purchases if there isn't a need for it.

Experiential Minimalists

An experiential minimalist tends to favor experiences more than buying things. Acquiring possessions doesn't hold much appeal for an experiential minimalist so an experiential minimalist might own only a few possessions and it is a symptom of their life and nothing more than that. They are the sorts who can easily fit their entire life into a backpack and will do so without any qualms. They tend to be adventure-seekers, travelers, explorers and digital nomads who like the idea of freelancing. They are the equivalent of a modern-day hippie.

Sustainable Minimalists

The sustainable minimalists are also known as the eco-minimalist. Their basic idea in life is to lead a life that's eco-friendly and environmentally sustainable. They like the idea of being able to reduce their dependency on things that can harm the environment. They want to lead a life that is sustainable for not just themselves, but the environment as well. Eco-minimalists like to lead a homestead life, or at least that's what they aspire to do. This lifestyle isn't about serving one's interests, but it is about not harming the environment. "Make do or make without" seems like the perfect motto for an eco-minimalist. This is the motto that an eco-minimalist uses to gauge their necessity for anything in their lives.

Thrifty Minimalist

All minimalists detest wastage, but thrifty minimalists dislike it even more. The waste-conscious habits of a thrifty minimalist are quite similar to those of sustainable minimalists, but the primary intention that motivates this type of minimalists is quite different. Their financial mindset prompts them to adapt to a minimalist lifestyle. A thrifty minimalist tries to make do with whatever they have, and they also try to limit their spending habits. They like to save and the only thing that tends to motivate them to save is their will to reduce their financial expenditure.

Mindful Minimalist

A mindful minimalist derives joy and even spiritual enlightenment whenever they get rid of unnecessary things from their life. The defining feature of this type of minimalist is sensible moderation. The only reason why mindful minimalists practice moderation is that it makes them happy and they don't it for any other environmental, financial or other aesthetic reasons. They do it purely for psychological reasons. A mindful minimalist obtains some peace of mind by letting go of all materialistic possessions. A mindful minimalist tries to maintain their peace of mind at all times and it is, in fact, quite dear to them. They try to not let any negative feelings bog them down. They get rid of all that is excess, and it allows them to be mindful.

Image Courtesy: Pixabay

Well, these are all the various types of minimalists. The one idea or philosophy that all minimalists agree on is their enthusiasm to get rid of all that is excess from their lives; however, the reasons and their motivation for doing this can vary.

Chapter Four

Embrace the Minimalist Lifestyle

In this section, you will learn about a couple of simple ways in which you can incorporate minimalism into your household.

Closets

It can be quite difficult to arrange or even rearrange closets. Usually, most of us tend to simply hold onto all those clothes that we no longer wear. Do you have certain items of clothing that you leave in your closet even when you dislike them, or you don't wear them? Well, in this section, you will learn about the ways in which you can use minimalism to reorganize your closet. The first thing that you must do is get rid of all those clothes that are torn. If something has holes in it, then please discard it. If you haven't worn something in a year, then you can perhaps donate it or sell it. Take a moment and think about it. If you didn't wear that item of clothing for a year, then it is quite unlikely that you will wear it now. If something doesn't seem to fit you or it is ill-fitting, then you can donate, sell or discard them. Please don't store them in your closet - they don't belong there!

How many clothes do you own, and how many do you need? Do you really need 15 pairs of jeans when all that you do is repeatedly wear those 5 pairs you prefer? Well, you certainly need to decide a number and then you need to stick to it as well. Once you decide the number, the next step is to make sure you have sufficient hangers to accommodate your clothes. For instance, if you decide that you need about 5 pairs of formal trousers, five pairs of jeans, five short-sleeved shirts, five long-sleeved shirts and about ten t-shirts, then make sure that you have sufficient hangers to accommodate all this. Go through your closet and pick those items of clothing that you cannot live without. When you do this, make sure that you keep the pre-decided limit in mind and please stick to that limit.

Do you really need 20 pairs of shoes? Do you need a trunk full of accessories? Well, the rules that apply to your clothes apply to all the accessories you own as well. Select only those things that you use and whatever you don't, you can get rid of them. The one thing that you need to keep in mind is that you need to stick to the essentials and, if something seems like its excess, then you need to get rid of it.

Kitchen

The kitchen is a very important part of any home. Here are a couple of tips that you can follow that will help reorganize your kitchen.

- Get rid of all those dishes that are either chipped or cracked.

- If you feel that you have too many coffee mugs or teacups, then keep a dozen of them and get rid of the rest.

- If you have any appliances or gadgets that you don't use, then you need to either give those away, or you need to get rid of them. If you have a food processor that you don't use daily, but you do use it a couple of times in a month, then hold onto it. If you have multiple copies of the same gadget or appliance, then you need to throw away all the duplicates. You don't need two toasters or two food processors, do you? For instance, if you have multiple sets of measuring cups, then you can certainly keep one set and remove the rest.

If you want, you can clear one portion of the kitchen at a time and not worry about decluttering the entire kitchen space at once. If you think you don't need something and are certain that you can replace it whenever you need it, please get rid of it. Also, check the cupboards for any food items that have expired or have gone bad. All the broken appliances, utensils or dishes, along with the expired food, need to go directly into the bin.

Toys

The rules of minimalism apply to every aspect of your child. Well, if you have any children at home, then the same rules apply to the toys they own as well. If there are certain toys that the children don't play with for a week or more, then you need to get rid of those toys. If your children are old enough, then they can make this decision by themselves. If you notice that something is broken or that the children have outgrown their toys, then you can donate them. If you cannot donate those toys or such, then you need to discard them. Whenever you need to purchase something for your children, opt for something that doesn't take up too much space. Keep in mind that the "quality is better than quantity" rule applies to their toys as well. If you notice that your children have a lot of stuffed animals, then you can keep a few, donate or throw away the rest. It is a good idea to donate toys and other things that your children no longer need. It might help someone else.

Bathrooms

You need to keep only those toiletries that you regularly use, and you don't need to have any other extras just lying around. If you don't use something, then you don't need it. You need a couple of towels and hand towels, but you don't need a closet stuffed with bathroom linen. Check the medicine cabinet and remove all the expired medicines. Call the local county government to dispose of any of the expired medicines. You need to get rid of all those products that have expired, and it means that you need to throw all the expired makeup products you might have in the cupboard. If there are any appliances that you don't use, then you need to get rid of them as well.

Living Area

If you want to live a minimalist lifestyle, then you need to get rid of all the clutter. If you think your living room is full of clutter, then it is time to declutter. Try to digitize your movies and music collection. Try to use technology to get rid of physical clutter. If you like to read, try to opt for eBooks and create a digital library to save some space. Alternatively, you can read books and then donate them, instead of holding onto them. Who doesn't like knick-knacks? However, you need to make sure that you reduce the number of knick-knacks that you have lying around the house. If something doesn't lend any value to you, then you don't need it.

These are just a couple of simple things that you can keep in mind whenever you decide to go down the minimalist route in your life. Minimalism is a constant work in progress. It means that you need to constantly and consciously try to prevent any clutter from creeping up in all aspects of your life.

Image Courtesy: Pixabay

Chapter Five

How to Live a Minimalist Life

Y ou might be of the opinion that the minimalist lifestyle isn't for everyone. In the world that we live in these days, people want to spend less, to do less and ultimately, to need less. If you want to do any of these things, then minimalism is the answer to all your problems. In this section, you will learn about the different steps that you can take to adopt a minimalist lifestyle.

Step One: Goal

Image Courtesy: Pixabay

You need to set a clear goal for yourself along with a timeline. According to you, what does a minimalist lifestyle mean or imply? Does it mean that you need to only possess the bare necessities? Does it mean that you need to declutter your home or workspace? Does it mean that you need to learn to live and not associate your happiness with purchasing new things? There isn't a fixed definition of minimalism. The concept of minimalism is quite subjective, and it can certainly differ from one person to another. Take some time and define what minimalism means to you. If you aren't certain about the things that you don't want, then make a list of the things that you do want. Make a list of all those things that make you happy, that make you feel alive, and the things that you are passionate about. Once you do this, then you can slowly discard everything else. You need to set a clear and specific goal for yourself. Once you set a goal, then you need to simplify this goal into smaller and simpler steps. Make it a point that you write down your goal and list all those steps that you can take to achieve the goal. Once you do this, the next thing that you need to do is establish a timeline to complete each of these steps.

Step Two: Your Home

You might consider moving into a smaller or a simplified home if you want to lead a minimalist lifestyle. If you rent or own a home, then this tip can be a major lifestyle overhaul; however, it certainly isn't an impossible thing to achieve. You need to think about your goal and you need to be very specific. If you aren't too sure of what you want, then you need to take some time and think about it. You can do some research, travel and even take a look at the kind of house that matches your ideology of minimalism. Minimalism doesn't mean that you always have to downsize, it merely means that you need to let go of all the things that you don't need.

Image Courtesy: Pixabay

Step Three: Declutter

You must declutter. It might sound like an obvious step, and it can be quite difficult for all those people who seem to be attached to all the things that they own. You need to start slow and don't try to declutter everything at once. It can feel a little overwhelming when you try to declutter initially but, after a while, it will not be that difficult. You need to understand that decluttering is a conscious decision and it is an ongoing process. All the things that you don't need, you can donate, sell or discard them. While you do this, you will realize that there are certain items that you cannot throw out, and you aren't sure whether you need them or not. Make sure that you place all these items in storage for a couple of months. If you can do without these items for a month or two, then you certainly don't need them. Initially, you might feel that you don't need something, and you get rid of it, only to realize that perhaps you were a little hasty. To avoid this, you need to place these items in storage so that you can gauge their importance. Minimalism doesn't mean that you need to throw everything away; instead, it merely means that you need to lead a lifestyle that helps you understand the importance of the things that you own. You don't need to fill your life with excess to live a happy life. Instead, you need to fill your life with things that matter to you, and do things that are important to you, if you want to live a meaningful life. You also need to understand that your idea of minimalism might or might not be the same as that of someone else so it is important that you understand what minimalism means to you before you decide to declutter.

Step Four: Train Yourself

It can take a while to get used to the minimal lifestyle, especially if you are a creature of comfort. You need to give yourself a little while and you must not rush into it. Take a couple of weeks or even a couple of months to slowly eliminate all the unnecessary comforts and luxuries that you are used to. You cannot get rushed into a minimalistic lifestyle, so take some time to ease your transition into it. You can start with something as simple as foregoing extravagant meals or pricey haircuts. You can keep all those things that make you happy. One thing that you need to remember is to not hold onto something, merely because you are used to having it around.

Step Five: Question

You need to constantly ask yourself "Do I need this?" Before you purchase anything, think about whether you need the item you are purchasing or not. Learn to differentiate between a need and a want. The basic necessities of any human being are food, clothing, shelter, security and love. Everything else that doesn't fall under these categories is a want. At first, you will try to justify all the purchases you make. Do you remember Isla Fischer's character from "The Confessions of a Shopaholic?" She had a hard time resisting the urge to purchase and, eventually, she was neck-deep in debt. Her inability to distinguish between wants and needs led to her bankruptcy so whenever you decide to buy something because it appeals to you, why don't you take a moment and ask yourself "Do I need this?"

Step Six: Re-Use

You need to learn to re-use. If you want to live like a minimalist, then you need to learn to re-use. Learn to fix or repair things instead of merely replacing them. For instance, you can fashion old glass bottles into vases. You can use old fabric for various DIY projects. A simple Google search will help you find multiple, easy-to-understand and simple ways to do DIY projects. Try to get creative about the ways in which you can re-use things around the house and avoid any unnecessary purchases. You can save money whenever you re-use something, but re-using doesn't mean that you start to horde things that "might" come in handy.

Step Seven: Always Opt for Quality

Image Courtesy: Pixabay

One of the primary principles of a minimalist lifestyle is that it is all about quality and not quantity. If you want to splurge, or if you want to purchase something, then you must always opt for a product that's of good quality and will last you long. It is better to own a couple of good-quality products instead of a cupboard full of cheap quality products that will not last you a month.

Step Eight: Clarity

The one thing that you must always do is revisit the first step. It means that you need to have clarity about what minimalism means to you and its implications on your life. It will help you concentrate on your goals.

If you want to adopt the lifestyle of a minimalist, then you need to be patient. Becoming a minimalist is a major lifestyle change and you need to give yourself some time to get used to thinking like a minimalist as well. It will take a while and don't expect to see any miracles overnight.

Chapter Six

Benefits of Minimalism

Minimalism offers certain benefits that you probably don't even know that you have been missing. Every benefit it offers is tied to the other so if you follow minimalism, it isn't about just one benefit that you will obtain, but all the benefits it offers. Some benefits will come easily to you, and the others depend on your level of acceptance of the minimalist lifestyle. Think about the minimalist mindset and the benefits it offers to decide your starting point and your goal you want to work towards.

Freedom

Image Courtesy: Pixabay

Minimalism offers the freedom that not only relates to your finances and personal peace, but it also relates to your ability to free up time to do the things that you enjoy. A materialistic lifestyle can hamper you. You probably tend to buy things even if there is no apparent reason to validate the purchase. You probably think, "This will look really good on the mantel" or "I have space for a couple of new pictures on the wall." These tendencies will disable you from being free to enjoy the things that you do love. Hobbies and travel can be quite expensive, especially from a financial viewpoint. If you want to spend small amounts like $2, $5, or $10 here and there, then you compromise your ability to free up your finances to do the things that you love. For instance, do you buy coffee every day on your way to work? $3 for a cup of coffee probably doesn't look like an expensive purchase but, if you spend $3 for your favorite coffee, you will spend about $15 every week and $60 in a month. It means that you spend around $720 for coffee every year. $720 is a lot of money and you probably never even think about it. Think about all the different ways in which you can spend this money. If you cannot do without your morning cup of coffee, then why don't you brew some coffee at home and carry it to work? Buying a packet of coffee powder or ground seeds is certainly cheaper than ordering coffee from your favorite joint. You can spend the money that you save on coffee on something that you love. You can perhaps fly to a new destination or spend that money on a hobby you enjoy. You can even pay off a debt. You will gain the financial freedom that's necessary to do something, or purchase something that you love.

Minimalism helps you free up some time from your daily schedule. What if you need to continuously work all month long to simply pay off your credit card bill? That doesn't sound good. In fact, it sounds quite tiring so, at the end of the month, all that you did was pay off your debt. A minimalist lifestyle will help you prioritize your tasks and you can concentrate on the things and activities that you like.

Worry-Free Living

Do you know that spending money can cause stress? In this world that's obsessed with materialism, people tend to agonize over the things that they cannot afford, that they don't have and the time that they don't have to do the things they love. All this agony can eat away at you. Minimalizing the way you live will give you the chance to have some peace of mind. Your stress will reduce, and you will worry less when you get rid of all the clutter in your life that tends to scare you.

What is the one thing that's worrying you right now? Are you worried about the next mortgage payment that's due? Does your credit card debt scare you? Do you worry that you are not able to spend sufficient time with your loved ones? Maybe you look at your home and think when you will find the time to organize and clean it? You might want to read a book and you cannot find the time to do so. Stress is self-induced, and all these worries can drive anyone insane so, if you adopt a minimalist approach to life, you can make peace with the things that you cannot do, and enjoy the things that you love. Love and peace of mind are two things that money cannot buy; however, you can attain these things, and minimalism helps you live a happier and a fulfilling life.

Health

When you are free of all the stress and you have time for yourself, your health will improve. Health is as much of a mental concept as it is a physical concept. Your physical health improves when you exercise, eat healthy meals and get rid of all the debilitating habits. Mental health improves when the stress you experience reduces. Minimalism helps reduce fear and stress.

What will you do if you have an hour to yourself? Imagine you don't have to worry about your bills, about cleaning or anything else. You will obviously feel more relaxed and calmer. Minimalism helps you relax, unwind and focus on the things that are important to improve your overall health.

Focus

How can you possibly concentrate on something when you have to think about a million things? We all like to think that we can easily multi-task, but do you think multi-tasking helps? How can you work on multiple things at once and not let it affect your productivity? For instance, can you talk over the phone and type something on your laptop simultaneously? Try doing it. Can you concentrate on the work as well as the phone call? Probably not, and you will realize that you did justice to neither of the tasks. That's because you only have a certain amount of focus and, when you try to multi-task, you spread yourself thin. Think of your focus as a bucket of water, and every thought you have is a hole in the bucket. How much water will be left in the bucket when it is full of holes? Not much focus will be left, and the same applies to your ability to multi-task. When you have less to think about, your ability to focus improves. If you want to be able to do your best, then you need to work on only one thing at a time. Whenever you declutter, you will be able to get rid of all the unnecessary distractions and, instead, concentrate on the things that do matter. When you have fewer worries, you will have more time and your focus will improve. You can work on things that matter to you and focus better.

Fear of Failure Reduces

Do you dread failure? Well, who doesn't? It is only human to be scared of failure. Fear of failure originates from having to do a lot and not having sufficient time to do it all. Do you understand how each of these benefits relates to the next one? It is not a linear equation and it is a codependent equation. If you restructure your life, then you can gain freedom, reduce the fear you experience and improve your focus. When you can do all this, the fear of failure reduces. Ask yourself the following questions:

What if you need to pay all your monthly expenses and all your debts? What will you do if you have no money left to have any fun? What if your debts are more than your income? What if you end up in bankruptcy or even foreclosure?

These what-if questions are merely an example of all the things that people seem to think of as failures. Not just this, but there are plenty of other fears that can scare a person. When your mind is full of such worries, your health will deteriorate, and you will not have sufficient time for yourself; however, you don't have to feel this way once you embrace a minimalist lifestyle. You can leave all these worries behind and concentrate on the things that you do enjoy.

Regain Values

Minimalism also helps shift the way you think. Human beings seem to think of themselves as an entitled species. We all seem to think that we are entitled to certain things in life, but are we really entitled to all that? Minimalism allows you to learn to be content with what you have in life and will prevent you from pining for things that you don't need. When you realize that your happiness comes from within, and that you cannot equate it with any other individual or any possession, that's when you will truly be happy. Imagine a world where everyone thinks like this. It might be the key to leading life in a harmonious and a happy manner.

Decluttering

If you want to lead a minimalist lifestyle, then you need to declutter. You need to streamline your life and focus on your goals. You can get rid of all the things that you didn't use in the last six months and only buy the things that are necessary. In your home, you can make more room or even downsize.

Image Courtesy: Pixabay

Chapter Seven

The Transition

At this point, you are probably thinking that you can become a minimalist. The benefits it offers sound wonderful and you can live a happier and a freer life but, how can you transition from your old habits to the minimalist life? There are numerous answers to this question. In fact, there is no right or wrong answer. Every person needs to transition in a manner that makes sense to him. You might look at a 21-day exercise schedule and think that you can follow it, but what will happen after those 21 days? Do you think you can continue on the path of minimalism even when you run into any obstacles? An important thing that you need to keep in mind when you transition into a minimalist lifestyle is to know your strengths and weaknesses. Usually, there are three categories within which all those who want to try the minimalist mindset fall under.

The first category consists of people who are ready to go – those who want to become a minimalist and are excited to declutter their lives, and the second category consists of all those who feel that they don't have sufficient space, not that they have a lot to fill that space with. The third category consists of all those who want to lead a minimalist life but aren't certain where to begin. Don't worry if you think that you don't fall under any of these categories, as there is no rule that you need to conform to them.

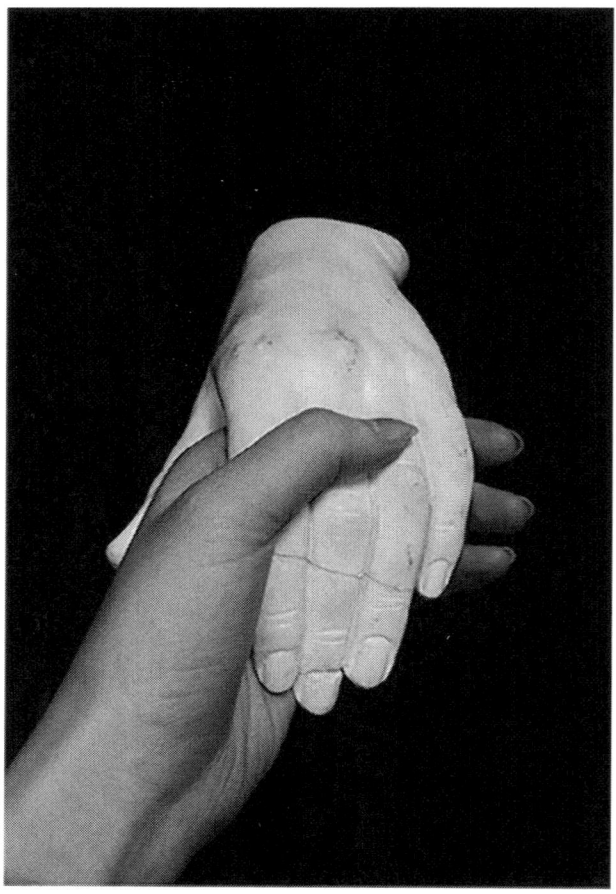

Any person who rushes into a decision without thinking things through will invariably falter at one point or the other during the transition. If you take some time to think about it all and slowly start the transition into minimalism, then your success rate will certainly be more than that of others. Again, you need to remember that there is no hard and fast rule about the ways in which you can change your life. Do whatever you think works best for you; however, the one thing that you need to remember is that the transition to minimalism doesn't happen overnight and you need to slowly work your way towards it.

Minimalism is a change in your lifestyle and it isn't a transition that you can make overnight. In fact, this is the main point where you need to evaluate your reality.

Do you have a partner? Do you have a spouse? Do you have children? Are there any other people who are an important part of your life or those that you live with? Does the thought of a change appeal to you, or does it fill you with dread? Can you ease into a change or does it make you cringe? Are you fine with the idea of experimenting before you find the level of minimalism that works well for you? Do you know what makes you happy? Can you accept that you will need to continuously try and define your life if you want to shift to minimalism?

The manner in which you answer the above-mentioned questions will determine whether you are willing to try the minimalist lifestyle or not. For all those people who have a spouse or a partner, then you need to make sure that he or she is fine with your decision to lead a minimalist life. If there are others involved in your life, then you need to make sure that all those involved are fine with your decision and will support you.

Steps You can Follow

In this section, you will learn about seven suggestions that you can incorporate if you want to lead a minimalist life.

Consider your reality, think about it for a while and come up with a plan that will work for you.

You need to select a room in your home that is free from all forms of clutter - the one room that is never messy. It is the one room that you can start with, and you can slowly work your way over to all the other rooms.

You need to make a conscious decision to get rid of all the duplicate items - it can be photographs, clothing, appliances or anything else that you can think of.

You can limit your wardrobe and try to come up with different combinations of clothes and the ways in which you can wear them.

Do you know that you can travel with fewer items? You certainly don't need a different swimsuit for each day that you spend in the Caribbean. Do you think you will go through more than three pairs of clothes when you are on a cruise for a couple of days? Also, you can always wash the clothes so you can travel with less.

You can simplify the time that you spend in the kitchen cooking and prepping meals if you change the way you cook. You can use a crockpot or cook one-pot dinners that will allow you to spend more time with your loved ones.

The final step in the process of transition is to make sure that you save about $1000. You can do this by tweaking your shopping habits. You need to buy less and learn to be happy without excess in life.

Discover Basic Steps

It is a common belief that you need about twenty-one days to form a new habit. To break your usual habits, you need to make certain that your brain can acclimatize itself to the concept of minimalism. The primary idea that the twenty-one steps approach professes is that when you give your brain a while to get used to this concept, then it becomes easier to transition to minimalism and even restructure your brain. Some people might need less than this and some might take a while longer; however, if you want to reduce the stress you experience, feel more confident and improve your overall success, then you need to try the twenty-one days approach. In fact, you can use this approach towards any change that you want to make in your life and not just minimalism. Here are the steps that you can follow:

The first step is to decide that you want to become a minimalist.

Start to separate all the things that you don't need from your general possessions.

You need to organize all the essential items.

Assess all the things that you own. You probably have some things that you have a sentimental or an emotional attachment with. Take a moment and reassess what those things mean to you. You can get rid of anything you want, provided you decide that you want to get rid of it.

Does the new lifestyle change scare you? If yes, then you need to re-examine this fear. Look at all the relationships in your life and all those people who always help you. You need to believe that you can change. If you don't believe this, then you cannot change.

You need to learn to grow as an individual. The things you love define you. When you try minimalism, you will be able to focus on the things that mean something to you. It will help you discover and understand yourself.

Now, take a pause and examine how you feel about all the steps so far.

You need to immediately get rid of all the trash.

Once you decide that you want to get rid of something, you can sell those items, if they can be sold.

If you cannot sell something and it is in good condition, then you can donate them.

You need to digitize certain aspects of your life if you want to declutter.

Re-examine all that you are left with after following all the above-mentioned steps. Do you think you can reduce your possessions further? If yes, then keep going.

Do you think you can move to a smaller home?

What are the things that you can change at your work to declutter and introduce minimalism to your work life?

Are there any specific areas of health that you can target?

Do you think you have too many electronic gadgets at home? Can you reduce the time that you spend watching television? Now that you have more time, you can organize and declutter your life. When you have all this spare time, what will you do to enjoy it?

These twenty-one steps will help you rethink the way your current life is and the things that you can change to achieve your goal of minimalism. There are no hard and fast rules about minimalism. You can do anything that you like, as long as you observe the principle of "less is more."

Your Psychology

What is your personality type? Before you decide to transition into the minimalist life, you need to know who you are. Are you the sort of person who does better with a couple of guidelines, or do you prefer to have a detailed plan?

The first thing that you need to do is take a look at your life at present. What if you have only six months to move out of your house? Did you shift three times in the last two years? Most of the times, it is quite easy to see the way in which you can become a minimalist if you have a different perspective. You probably move around a lot, but do you start to regain things the minute you start to settle down?

For instance, one family had to deal with different struggles within a span of five years. It all started with a move because of health issues that turned into four moves in three years for a family member. Another family of four had to face the struggles of bankruptcy and divorce. The family had to endure the struggle of a custody battle that resulted in another move.

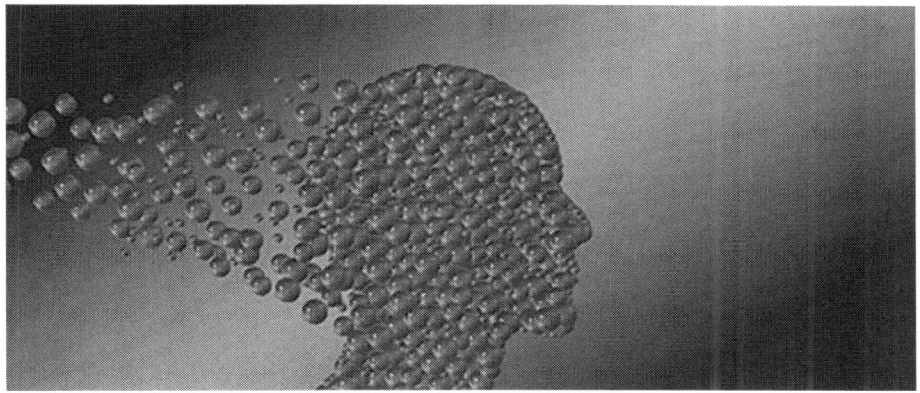

You never know how you will deal with a situation until that situation comes up. If you really want something, then you will find a way to make it happen. The first step is to assess your life and think about the way it is. Take a moment and think about the things or events that shaped your life and any of the other potential changes that you might need to make. According to you, what is the hardest thing that you had to face in life so far? There can be no right or wrong answer to this question. For one person it can be the loss of a pet, an illness, the loss of a loved one or even the loss of a job. What might seem like a difficult situation for one might not be the same for someone else.

When faced with a difficulty, how did you deal with it? In retrospect, do you think you there is something that you will probably like to change? If a similar situation crops up in the future, do you think you will deal with it in the same manner, or will you change something about it? We all tend to react differently to different events in life. All the major events in your life will give you a glimpse of your personality. You might probably think that you have hit rock bottom with one event until something else comes along your way. In comparison, you will realize that probably life isn't as bad as you seem to think because you still have things that you value. The point is that you need to assess who you are at present, your limits and then try to think of the ways in which you can adopt a minimalist mindset. Right now, you might think that you don't know how to transition or that you don't know how to stick to a minimalist lifestyle if something goes wrong. You will only know what your reaction to a situation will be when the said situation takes place. You might have a couple of plans about what a favorable reaction needs to be like; however, all this doesn't matter when something happens.

Like mentioned earlier, a minimalistic lifestyle is not a destination, but it is an ongoing journey that will guide you through life. If you can understand this simple statement, then you can slowly transition into the new lifestyle according to your psychological traits. Along the way, you will also learn a lot about yourself. You need to look forward to all the changes that come along with minimalism, and you need to embrace all that you discover.

Chapter Eight

What Matters the Most to You?

Minimalism helps you shift your focus to the things that you love and helps you let go of everything else, but how can you decide on what is important to you and what isn't? In this chapter, you will learn about the different questions that you can ask yourself to evaluate your priorities in life.

Minimalism and Goal Setting

Does the idea of minimalism appeal to you, but you are not sure where you need to start? Well, the primary reason why a lot of people are excited about the concept of minimalism is that of the overwhelming lives we lead these days. Minimalism helps make your life more manageable. The first step that you need to take if you want to try minimalism is to understand where you can start. You can cultivate helpful habits only when you know where to start.

Image Courtesy: Pixabay

If simplification is your goal, then you need to understand the relationship that exists between physical clutter and emotional clutter. When you start to get rid of all sorts of physical clutter from your surroundings, then you can concentrate on removing all emotional clutter as well. There are four simple steps that you can follow if you want to set a goal for yourself.

Step One: Your Goal

Before you can work on anything in your life, you need to understand your goals. The same logic applies to minimalism as well. You need to identify your goal and then understand the manner in which it relates to your life in general. Take some time out of your schedule and think of the reasons why you need a goal and then start to prep for the journey towards minimalism. If you don't have a goal, then it is likely that you will not make any real progress. You might make a couple of half-hearted attempts to try minimalism but, without a goal, you will not be able to make any real progress. Minimalism is not a radical or a restrictive lifestyle. In fact, it means to live a happy and satisfied life.

Step Two: Don't Hold Yourself Back

Do you set goals for yourself from time to time? Do you tell others about the goal as soon as you make one? After a while, do you lose steam and forget about your target and move onto something else? If your answer is yes, then you need to think about all those instances in the past where you established a goal but did not achieve it. You need to avoid all the mistakes that you made in the past. Think about all the various factors that were holding you back, and you need to try to find a way to work around it. Usually, there are two main factors that prevent people from achieving their goals. These two factors are perfectionism and self-doubt or self-acceptance. Perfection is quite an alluring idea. Most of us tend to waste all our time trying to chase perfection. In fact, there is nothing in this world that is perfect and you need to make your peace with it, so stop chasing perfection. The more you chase perfection, the more elusive it will seem and the farther away you will be from your goal! Take a moment and take a deep breath. Perfectionism will hinder you from taking any action whatsoever because, the more you think about an idea, the more problems you will seem to think about and more changes you will make. When you do all this, you forget about a major step and that is taking action so, instead of trying to start something perfect, take a breath and just take the first step. Only when you start will you know the course of action that you need to take to achieve your goal. Any action that you take is better than merely wondering whether it will be perfect or not.

The next obstacle that a lot of people face is their inability to accept themselves. If you want to change something, then before you can make any of the changes, you need to learn to accept yourself. Did you see a rocking chair and did you ever notice the way it moves? Once it gains a little momentum, it doesn't stop. Well, stress works in a similar manner. Once the stress sets in, you will continuously start to worry about something or the other. There is no end to it unless you consciously make a decision to stop worrying.

Familiarity brings comfort and it is quite easy to become comfortable with the things that are familiar. On the other hand, the unknown can be quite scary. When you finally learn to let go of things and learn to accept where you are in life, it is quite easy to deal with the outcomes.

Change need not be scary, and it is quite essential for growth. If you want to grow in life, then you cannot be dormant. Change doesn't seem too scary when you start to think of it as an adventure. Even all those who don't seem confident can get scared every now and then.

Whenever you feel that you are starting to worry about the future, you need to simply remind yourself that no-one can predict the future. You never know what is in store for you and you certainly cannot predict it. There can be times when you imagine the absolute worst, but the outcome isn't as bad as you anticipated and vice versa. You need to accept that you need to live in the present and let your destiny guide you.

You need to learn to be confident about yourself. Don't try to indulge in any superficial things to mask any self-doubt. You need to learn to accept yourself and understand that life isn't about the materialistic things. Minimalism will help change your perspective towards things, as well as people.

Step Three: Visualization

Always think about the big picture. This step goes together with the first step mentioned. You need to be able to visualize what success means to you and what it looks like. If you cannot visualize your goal, then you need to reconsider your goal. Try to be as descriptive about your visualization as possible. Talk to yourself about how amazing it will be to achieve your goal. The clearer and detailed the visualization is, the more excited you will be to achieve that goal.

Step Four: Plan of Action

Once you are certain of your goal, then you need to devise a plan of action. If you don't take any action to achieve your goal, it will merely stay a dream. If you want to achieve your goal, then you need to plan the steps that you need to take to achieve that goal. It means that you need to be able to motivate yourself to keep going even when you feel like giving up. A plan will help you focus and help you use your energy to achieve your priorities.

Additional Tips

Here are some additional tips that you can use to set goals for yourself:

Start with an "Ideal" Situation

Now is your chance to dream and you must dream big. Imagine that you have a blank slate in front of you and you can decide who you want to be or what you want to do. Don't worry about all the possible hurdles immediately, just focus on all your dreams for now. There might be different things that you want to do in your life. Start with all the different possibilities and then you can move onto the practicality and viability of those ideas. Yes, don't worry about all the bills, the debts, or other burdens while you are dreaming. Think about the idyllic version of "you" and then you will start thinking of the different ways in which you can transform it into reality.

Start Writing Down Your Goals

Image Courtesy: Pixabay

Once you have thought about your goals, the next step is to write down these goals. Making a note of your goals will help you to start seeing the direction you must head in, and this, in turn, simplifies the process of decision-making. This does sound old school, doesn't it, but writing down your goals is very helpful. People usually like keeping everything in their brain instead of writing it down. When you write something down, it provides a sense of clarity. Once you have written down your goal or goals, place that sheet such that you will be able to see it daily. If you want, you can even make multiple copies of it! Place a copy of it on your cupboard door or the bathroom mirror. It will keep reminding you and will also encourage you to start thinking about your goal. Repeated exposure assists in focusing your conscious and subconscious mind on the things you want to achieve in life.

Determine their Importance

You need to have clarity when it comes to setting goals for yourself. Why is that goal significant to you? Does it hold significance because your loved ones want you to do it, or because you want to do it for yourself? Make sure that the goals you are setting for yourself aren't any of the "must-be" ones. If you start thinking about all the things that you must and must not be doing according to others, then the list will be an endless one. Instead, start thinking about the things that you want to do for yourself. For instance, your goal is to lose weight and get your body in shape. Now, think about the reasons why this is important for you? Are you willing to take the necessary steps and make those necessary sacrifices for attaining this goal? We must often make difficult choices while setting specific goals. It is a natural part of the process so you will need to start prioritizing. Will you or won't you feel a sense of achievement when you achieve the goal? That's the primary question you need to be able to answer while thinking about your goals. For instance, you might be thinking about becoming the best business in a niche market and, at the same time, you want to be able to spend a lot of time with your child and coach your child's basketball team. In such a case, it can happen that you don't necessarily feel happy after achieving your goal.

Even if the questions seem quite tough, you have to consider them. Sit down and start brainstorming for different ideas and alternatives. Don't worry about what you are writing; just write everything down that you can probably think of. Here are a couple of questions that will help you in this process:

What will I do if I only have a month left to live? What will I do if I have all the money I need? What will I do if I knew that I would never fail?

Once you have successfully answered these questions, forget about it all for 24 hours. Come back after a day and see if you still feel the same about the things that you have written down. If you do, then you have your answer!

Your Goals Must Add Some Meaning to Your Life

A goal must never be vague. If it is vague, you will never be able to achieve it. If you want to exercise frequently or maybe become a better leader, then your goal needs to be very specific. Try saying your goal out loud and be honest with yourself about whether it has some clarity or not. Once you have clarity, then you have to ensure that it is something that you genuinely care about. Goals might seem specific, but they are in fact, quite vague. For instance, a goal that says getting in shape isn't a specific one. It can imply a reduction in your cholesterol levels, losing excess weight, improving your overall stamina, or even your ability to run a marathon. Getting in shape is quite vague. Instead, a goal like "I want to lose 20 pounds in 3 months" is specific. If you don't want to abandon your goal, make sure that it isn't a vague one.

Prioritize and Pursue Your Goal

It is very likely that you will have a lot of vital things in your life so make a list of all your goals and then select the three most important ones from the list. These three goals are your tier-one goals: the goals that have the potential of altering your life. They aren't necessarily the goals that will help you make money or anything of that sort, but they are the goals that will lend some meaning to your life. These goals can be big or small and can be something like changing your profession, completing your college, or paying off your student loans. The only condition is that the goals mentioned in tier-one must be of some significance to you.

Setting a Target Date

Image Courtesy: Pixabay

It might be quite difficult, but you need to do it. Listing down a specific goal is just one step, and it doesn't amount to anything without a target date or a deadline for achieving it. For instance, if you have set a goal "I want to lose 15 pounds" isn't as specific as something that says, "I want to lose 15 pounds within three months". Setting a deadline gives you a target to work with. When you don't set a deadline for yourself, it is very likely that you will end up procrastinating. Procrastinating is a basic human tendency, and, without a target, you will not achieve your target and, not just that, having a target also allows you to measure your progress and adjust the pace at which you are going.

Taking Small Steps

You don't need to do everything at once. Take it slow and steady. Once you have managed to finalize on a goal, the next step is to start taking small steps that will help you achieve your goal. One small step a day can help you achieve great results. Achieving your goals is a process and not magic, so it does take a while. You can create a one-step-a-day rule for yourself. It means that every day, you will be doing something, regardless of how big or small it is that will help you in achieving your goals.

Less is More

The more goals that you have, the less time and energy you will have at your disposal for each one, so it will be wise to limit the number of goals that you have set for yourself. One single goal will be great because it means that you will be able to dedicate all your time, energy, and focus towards that one goal.

If you want to set goals for yourself to achieve minimalism, then you need to follow the simple steps discussed in this section.

Chapter Nine

Self-Assessment

If you aren't certain of what is important to you, then you need to make a list of all the things that you love. Minimalism isn't about merely cutting things out of your life, or about creating a void in your life. Minimalism is all about shifting your focus and energy towards the things that you enjoy. It is about eliminating all forms of clutter to make space for the things you love. The first objective of minimalism is to identify the things that are important to you. All the physical and emotional clutter that we surround ourselves with tends to make us feel quite overwhelmed. Not just that, in this world that is obsessed with materialism, all the excess we surround ourselves with can distract anyone from their goals. If you want to lead your life like this, then minimalism is the answer for you. A life that is unexamined is a life that isn't worth living. You need to examine your life if you want to simplify it. There are certain questions that you can ask yourself to understand all your needs. In this section, you will learn about the different questions that you can ask yourself to identify the things you love. Apart from this, you will also learn about the way in which you can identify your passion. Only when you know the answers to these questions can you think about minimalism.

Image Courtesy: Pixabay

Question #1

You need to determine what you love. To do this, you can ask yourself "What do I love the most?" or "What is the one thing that means the most to me?" Your answers to these questions will help you understand your priorities in life, and the answers will obviously differ from one person to the next. In fact, there is no such thing as a right or a wrong answer to this question. For some people, it might be important to spend time with their loved ones, and, for some, it might be their love for traveling or any hobby that they enjoy. Before you can transition into minimalism, you need to understand what you love. You will learn more about this later on in the chapter.

Question #2

The next thing you need to determine is the things that you do daily, and the way in which they correlate to the previous question. Ask yourself "What are the different things that are going on in my life and the manner in which these things relate to what is important to me?" For instance, do you tend to go out for drinks with your friends once a week, but you don't think that this is important? If that's the case, then you can stop doing it and instead do something else. You can spend all the time that you spend on going out for drinks with your friends on something that you actually enjoy. Take some time and evaluate your commitments. Then you can understand the things that are really important to you, and the ones that are not.

Question #3

The third aspect of your life that you need to analyze is about the things that you own. You need to think about all your possessions. Ask yourself whether you love everything that you possess or not. Do you love all your possessions and do they all hold the same level of importance as the rest? There is a simple manner by which you can determine what you love. For instance, if your house burns down, what are all the things that you can replace? If you can replace something, it means that you don't love it. So, the answer to this question will help you determine the importance of possessions. Once you have your answer, you can hold onto the things that you love and then get rid of everything else. When you get rid of all the clutter, you will be left with only the things that you love.

Question #4

If you want to determine the value of everything else in your life, then apply the logic that you used to determine the answer to the previous question. For instance, you are probably surrounded by a lot of people daily; however, in your time of need, whom do you depend on? If you were stuck in a crisis, whom do you call? The ones that you depend on during your time of need are the ones that you love. The rest are just acquaintances. It is perfectly all right to have a small circle of close friends who are dependable, trustworthy and loyal, instead of surrounding yourself with a lot of people. Once you can differentiate between those people you care for and the ones that are mere acquaintances, you can spend your time with them accordingly.

Question #5

Where do you spend most of your time? What are the things that you spend your time on? You can use these questions to understand the things that you love and the things that matter to you. Do you spend a lot of time reading, watching TV or working on your laptop? The time that you invest in people, as well as the things you do, will determine their importance.

Question #6

Another thing that will help you determine what you love is the way you handle your finances. What are the things that you spend your money on? Where do you spend your money? Perhaps you like to buy clothes, travel or even invest. Your spending habits will help you analyze your life and think about the things that you love.

Question #7

Think about all the thoughts you spend a lot of time on. What do you think about? If you are sitting by yourself, then what are the things that you think about? Do you think about someone or something? Your thoughts can also help you understand what you love. If you realize that you spend most of your time thinking about things that don't really matter, then it is time that you do something about it. Usually, wherever your thoughts go, your heart tends to follow.

Question #8

If you had just one day to live, then what will you do on that day? For instance, if today is the last day of your life, what will you do? Your mind will automatically think about all the things that you value a lot in your life. There are certain aspects of your life that are important and then there are those that aren't.

How to Decide what's Important to You?

While running a marathon, if you sprint for the first 100 meters, it is likely that you will tire yourself out. Well, most of us seem to treat our goals in the same manner. It might be patience, passion, or even willpower that might be lacking. Itis likely that most of us don't attain success because we just do not understand the formula for success. A formula doesn't have to mean a complicated scientific formula. It can be simplified into seven basic principles that will help you achieve the success you have always dreamt of.

Image Courtesy: Pixabay

The human mind is quite powerful, and it creates our reality. The existence that we experience, all that we perceive, and all the thoughts that we have, they all exist in our mind and only in our mind. Our mind is capable of experiencing the same thing in a different manner at different times. All the different sounds, colors, sights, interactions, and memories that we experience will affect each of us differently, and the way we interpret them is different as well. Our perception of the world is entirely different as well, and not everyone will have the same interpretation. From our birth, we start to experience things and form descriptions that help us build the bubble that we live in, and it develops our version of reality. Everyone has a different version of reality and the way that things are. Luckily, our minds are so influential that we can create an ideal world for ourselves. It is possible to ignore all the evil that exists in this world and still shape it to fit our idea of perfection. Well, it might sound slightly delusional, but it isn't. Our mind is an extremely powerful tool, and when you unlock its true potential, you can achieve greatness. There are a couple of similar qualities that all successful people tend to share, regardless of the area in which they have achieved success. If you want to be successful, you need to be passionate about it. You need to be so passionate about something that it seems like you are almost obsessed with it. Obsession is usually considered to be quite unhealthy, but it doesn't necessarily have to be something unhealthy. In fact, a healthy obsession is similar to understanding your purpose of living. We are all either searching for our passion or are already working on fulfilling it. A healthy obsession is one of the essential steps to achieving success in any filed. It is said that it takes about 10,000 hours of practice for mastering a skill or craft, for understanding and grasping it. Persistence is essential for understanding something. An unwavering interest and ability to focus on something are what obsession is all about.

However, it is essential to find a healthy obsession and not an unhealthy one. A healthy obsession is something that you are not only passionate about, but something that benefits you as well. Some might argue that finding a passion that is selfish will do the trick; however, a negative obsession doesn't generate any positive results. You need to find an obsession that will not only make you happy, but will also enable you to improve your life without making you feel any guilt. Being obsessed is the only way in which you can become successful and stay ahead of the game. Obsession is a trait that distinguishes leaders from the followers. Like mentioned earlier, our mind is quite complicated, and it holds complete power over itself. It runs itself, but you can control it as well. Sufficient repetition and focus can help change the manner in which your mind perceives and interprets things. To a certain extent, you can even adjust the manner in which your mind sees and understands things. By changing your perception of the world, you can start working on influencing and changing things for the better.

If you want to be passionate to the extent of being obsessed, then the first step is to find something that you are in love with. Something that provides you with a sense of direction. Finding your passion might take some time and you cannot force it. If you want to see your passion, then you need to be patient and have an open mind. It isn't something that you can learn; it has to come to you. Most of us tend to find something that we are passionate about, but not many of us follow our passions. We tend to choose not to feed the embers. Just like love, passion is lost when you don't keep it alive. It is a misconceived notion that your life will merely unfold for you if you find something that you are passionate about. Nothing happens unless you make it happen. You can start prioritizing the tasks on hand when you find something that you are passionate about. That's when you realize that it is rational to spend all your time working on something that you are passionate about, and the things you love, instead of insignificant work. After that, it's just the matter of putting in the necessary working hours. There will be no result if you don't put in the necessary effort. It includes researching, planning, and acting on it. You will have to force yourself to concentrate on your passion whenever you possibly can. Whenever you have nothing to work on, or you find your mind wandering, think about your passion. Think about the thing you are trying to accomplish - the goal you are trying to achieve - as much and for as long as you can. Think about your goals before going to bed and the first thing after you wake up. You can work on your passion by letting go of all the unnecessary distractions and by focusing on the things that matter. If you are passionate about something, then you will enjoy every moment of the journey you are taking, even the less-enjoyable moments won't seem that bad. When you start enjoying what you are doing, you will love it, and you will find that it gets easier to devote your energy towards working on it quite easily. Initially, you will have to force yourself to concentrate on it, and eventually, you will not have to do that, and the concentration you need will come naturally to you. However, you need to remember that it is the healthy obsession that's desirable and not the unhealthy sorts. A healthy obsession will provide you with the necessary focus to avoid all sorts of distractions, and you will notice your progress.

Passion is essential for attaining success, but how do you decide about the things that you are passionate about? Whether you are trying to find a career that excites you, or a hobby that enriches your life, finding a passion is instinctual. Passion is a critical component of the overall psychological wellbeing of an individual and his or her ability to accomplish goals. In this section, you will learn about certain questions that will help you find your true passion.

What Interested You during Your Younger Days?

What was the one thing that you were always excited to do when you were young? What was the topic of your thesis in your senior year in high school? Was there a particular hobby that you were inclined towards?

What Causes do You Care About?

Knowingly or unknowingly, you end up developing a soft spot for a couple of causes. Think about all those causes that you care for. It can be a fund for supporting students from backward areas, a fund for research on cancer, and pretty much anything. You just need to find a cause that excites and motivates you.

Do Something Scary

Whenever you feel like you are unsure of what you are doing in life, then a simple manner in which you can pull yourself out of the rut is by doing something scary. No, it doesn't mean that you need to join an extremist organization or anything of that sort. It just means that you must do something that scares you. Minimalism is all about doing things that matter to you. It usually happens that the things that we love a lot tend to scare us. If you are scared to quit your job to work towards your dream, then the first step is to understand your passion and then pursue it.

Forget about Finances, for a While

If you feel like you aren't able to find your passion, forget about the financial aspect involved in it for a while. Forget about making money and all the debts involved. If you have all the money you need, and you can focus on one thing, what will that thing be? Doing this will help you understand your passion.

Passion is essential for your overall wellbeing and for achieving your goals as well. Passion is the fire that will keep you going and provide you with the healthy obsession that is desirable. We are all faced with numerous decisions daily, regardless of our age and profession, but not every decision is an important one. For instance, deciding on what your next meal must be isn't as important as figuring out your career options. Learn to differentiate between those that are important and those that aren't. Start prioritizing your tasks and spend more time while deciding something of significance.

Have you ever heard of Bobby Fischer? Yes, the greatest chess player of all time! He is a perfect example of someone who was obsessed with the game. Fischer studied harder than any of the other players; he used to wake up in the morning and go to bed thinking about chess. Why did he keep doing this? It wasn't just about being a great chess player; Bobby wanted to be the best chess player ever. That was his only dream, and he committed himself to it. He was obsessed with achieving greatness, and it is that obsession that gave him the necessary motivation to keep going.

Michael Jordan, without a doubt, is the greatest basketball player on Earth, and no-one ever trained harder than Jordan did. Jordan never liked mediocrity and always wanted to excel at whatever he did. He never gave anything less than his absolute best, and that's why he is the best. Larry Bird summed up this attitude of Jordan's in an incredible manner in his autobiography. While growing up, Jordan always felt that he was behind and that he needed some extra hours to catch up with others. Jim Jones told Jordan that regardless of the number of shots he took, there will be someone out there who took a shot more than him and dribble a couple of times more than he did. Whenever Jordan felt that he was ready to call it a day, he used to stop himself and work for a while longer. In his mind, there was always a possibility that someone will work more than he did. His passion was playing basketball, and he did everything he can to turn that passion into his life.

If you find something that you want to do, and you want to find success while doing it, then you need to be obsessed with it healthily.

Chapter Ten

Happiness and Minimalism

Happiness can be a significant motivational factor, but did you know that just one out of three people could say that they are happy? Think about it. How often do you complain about being stuck in a queue at the airport while boarding? Do you complain when your flight gets delayed? Well, we all do that, and these complaints are quite common. It feels like we all might have taken a simple fact for granted - human beings can fly now! How incredible is that? How can we feel sick of these beautiful things already? Why is it so easy to complain and thus tricky to appreciate? Isn't it easier to concentrate on the negative aspects of your life instead of the positive ones? You don't need anything to be fancy. A happy person can control their emotions and will not let their emotions dictate their lives. If you aren't satisfied with yourself, then you cannot blame anyone else other than from yourself. Do you feel better if you can blame someone else for your lack of happiness? Bad things happen to everyone, without any discrimination. Life isn't about what happens; it is mostly defined by the manner in which you react to all these situations.

Image Courtesy: Pixabay

Happiness and minimalism go hand in hand. Minimalism will help you live a happier life. In this section, you will learn about a couple of behaviors that will help you feel happy all the time.

The Need for Specific Outcomes

You might have grand plans in life, but not everything will necessarily go according to it. Setbacks are quite common, and things might or might not happen. You might mess something up and obsessing over it will not help you. Concentrating too much on things will make your happiness dependent on the outcome, and this attitude will not do you much good. When you want a specific outcome, you are unknowingly sabotaging yourself. If the outcome isn't what you expected, you will feel sad regardless of whether the outcome is good or bad.

Defining Your Success

No two human beings are alike, so why must we all have one standard to measure success? All of us end up getting stuck in the rat race that the society has created towards achieving the so-called standard of "success" that are set by the community. There will always be someone that's better than you at something or the other. There will never be sufficient time to do everything. Instead, you need to focus on the things you opt for. When you select something, you have simultaneously rejected something else. It is the norm of life, and it is entirely alright to do so. It is quite pleasant how we get to choose what we want. You will need to define what happiness, success, and wealth mean to you. You cannot let society decide what you need, or think you need. If that's the case, then you will always fall short of something or the other. You will need to stop comparing yourself to others and stop competing with others. It is the only manner in which you will get ahead in life. Pull yourself out of the endless rat race and the rut that you are stuck in.

Commit Yourself to Things that Make You Happy

How many times have you told yourself "just this once"? Most of us have convinced ourselves that we are capable of breaking our own rules. We will always find reasons to justify these small choices we make. None of these things feel like a significant decision initially, but, over a period, these things end up forming a part of the bigger picture. Human beings are good at sabotaging themselves. People tend to behave in a manner that goes against their goals or their ideals. The gap between what you do, and what you must do, needs to be as small as possible. The lower this difference is, the happier you will be in life. Giving 100% commitment is more comfortable than giving 98%. When you have committed yourself fully to something, then this means that the decision has already been made. Unless and until you are fully committed to something, you will always end up being a victim of all the external circumstances in life. If you only rely on your willpower, it is more likely that you will end up crumbling. You might think that you are doing better than what you are doing. You needn't rely on your willpower once you have given your 100% commitment. Regardless of the circumstances, your decision has been made. It is all about being proactive instead of being reactive.

Grateful

Image Courtesy: Pixabay

Being grateful can be termed as focusing your energy on what you have in your life instead of focusing on the things that are missing. Happiness is an elementary concept, and it can be as simple as gratitude that you feel. According to research, there are specific physical, psychological, and social benefits of feeling gratitude. These interests include a stronger immune system, reduction in body aches and pains, better blood pressure, and better sleep too. The psychological benefits are increased feelings of positivity; you'll feel more alert, experience more joy, and be optimistic. The social benefits are that you will feel more helpful, generous, compassionate, forgiving, outgoing, and less isolated. In spite of all these benefits, most people are usually ungrateful. People tend to focus too much of their time and attention on what they don't have. The grass always does seem greener on the other side. If it was one thing that you wanted, after achieving it, it will be something else. There is no end to this ever-growing list of wants. Life has become a constant race for having the best of things. How can you ever be happy when all you want from life is more things? Take a moment and appreciate what you have. Only when you can count your blessings, will you realize how fortunate you are.

Human beings, in general, need to learn to be more grateful. Your happiness depends on your ability to be thankful. Here are a few things that you can do to be more grateful. You can maintain a gratitude journal. Fill this up with instances of moments of sincere gratitude associated with the most commonplace events that take place. It will help you feel more grateful. Think about all the challenges that you have overcome in life. It will help you feel thankful for what you have in life. You cannot honestly embrace what you have in life if you don't remember the struggle you went through to get what you have. Here are a few questions that you can ask yourself that'll help you with self-introspection. Ask yourself, what you have received from, given to, and the troubles you have caused. These questions will help to provide your life with some perspective, and you will start looking at things from a different perspective. You can learn a few prayers of gratitude as well.

Language

Be conscious of the language that you make use of. People who are grateful make use of different words like gifts, abundance, blessings, fortune, fortunate, and blessed more frequently. If you start incorporating these words into your daily vocabulary, you will realize that the list of things that you need to be grateful for keeps on increasing. It will allow you to understand and appreciate the abundance that is present all around you. Smile a lot and say thank you when someone does something for you. It can be something as simple as thanking someone for holding the door open for you.

It might sound strange. Try saying, "I love you" to your friends and family members. They will all be pleasantly surprised; however, make sure that you are sincere while saying this. Saying these three simple words will not only change the person to whom you have spoken this to, but it will change you as well. By merely saying these words, you will feel more love towards that person. It is essential for others to know that they are valued and cherished. Do it today.

You needn't wait until tomorrow for something that you can do today. Happiness is all about embracing the present that we live in. It is about not letting that moment just pass by. Never miss out on the essential things in life for something that you think is "important." What you might think will impress someone might just be considered to be a flaw in your character. Get rid of all the things that are not essential or vital to your being. There is nothing in this life that can be considered to be permanent. Everything is transient. Children grow up, friends tend to move away, and our loved ones pass on to the other side. Always live in the present. Don't forget to appreciate what you have in life, so take the time to enjoy the things you cherish, before it is too late.

Doing Something that Scares You

Image Courtesy: Pixabay

You will need to step out of your comfort zone if you want to grow in life. A happy person is comfortable outside their comfort zone. You will need to challenge yourself to develop. Growth is a significant prerequisite for happiness. If you aren't growing and improving, then you are becoming stagnant and are decaying. Taking a risk will make you feel alive, and it will put you in a state of consciousness that will enable you to perform to the best of your ability. You will become thoroughly engaged in what you are doing. When you are doing things that are outside your comfort zone, then you will improve your conscious level as well. The probability of failure will force you to think better and differently from your usual routine. Your mind will be forced to get creative and innovative. Sadly, most people tend to play safely in life. Their goals are usually logical. There is little or no element of risk that is involved. You need to take chances in life. Do those things that make you feel alive. Activate the energy within you. Of course, when there are risks involved, there will be failures too. Don't think of a failure at the end. It is just a temporary setback, and it can be easily overcome. There is no need to give up. Experience the good and the bad in life. This is the only way in which you will grow. Promise yourself that you will do all those things that scare you. Take them one at a time.

"Important" and "Urgent"

Most of the time people end up spending their time on things that are urgent, even though they are unimportant. We wake up in the morning, and the first thing that we do is check our messages or emails. We have programmed ourselves to be reactive instead of being proactive. A happy person will always make the important things a priority. Not just urgent, but essential and non-urgent things as well. The things you must focus on can be exercising, reading essential books, setting goals for yourself, writing a journal, and spending time with your loved ones. None of those above-mentioned things are urgent; however, these things are essential. These things can be quickly put on hold until the next day, and they usually get postponed. The happy and prosperous people in the world tend to spend most of their time on the things that are important.

110

One way in which you can do this will be by waking up early in the morning. Establish a morning routine for yourself. You can meditate or exercise, go for a jog, play with your pet, or do something that you enjoy. This will make you feel positive about the rest of the day, and keep you motivated as well.

There are a lot of things in life that are good, and even great. It doesn't mean that you must do them all. Every day, you are faced with once-in-a-lifetime opportunities. Most people tend to grab onto any great opportunity that comes their way, even though it is not in synchronization with their vision in life. This is the reason why the lives of people tend to move in different directions. They can't run in a single direction on a conscious level. On the contrary, a happy person will refuse the incredible opportunity as well. They will not want to sacrifice their freedom for the sake of security. They will not let distractions divert their attention. There are only excellent things in life that can be described as the very "best". You are the only one that gets to decide what's best for you. Don't keep yourself occupied with the so-called "good" activities and miss out on the amazing ones. Learn to enjoy life.

Chapter Eleven

Life without Clutter

A process that comes in handy in your personal, as well as professional life is decluttering. It is also a part of the process of minimalism. In this section, you will learn about decluttering. Decluttering helps you streamline your life and work, as well as your emotions. If you want to declutter, then you need to assess different aspects of your life. When you start to declutter, you will realize that you don't need plenty of things to be happy. It will help you understand that "less means more". There are a couple of things that you need to keep in mind when you assess your life and work. The one question that all minimalists ask themselves is whether something holds value or not. We are not talking about the financial value of things, but things that lend meaning to your life. Something can seem like junk to one person and can be priceless to someone else. The art of decluttering will help you examine what you own and how much of your time it takes up. You can categorize your life into three categories and a couple of subcategories. You have a personal and a professional life. Work helps you earn your living and help you understand your talents. It gives you the motivation to wake up in the morning and move beyond merely living.

Image Courtesy: Pixabay

When you take this out of the equation, then all that you are left with is your personal life; therefore, the three main categories in your life are work, personal life and emotional life. Of course, you need to work on emotional clutter as well, and that's the reason why it is discussed beyond your personal life. You need to learn to not let each of these categories clash with others. You need to learn to separate your emotional life from your personal life and vice versa.

Personal Life

In this section, you will learn about the different aspects of decluttering that relate to your personal life.

House

There are lots of myths about minimalism, and one of the popular myths is that minimalism is about decluttering and reducing your home, but it doesn't have to be. It is just one aspect. Your house is a small portion of your personal life. Let us examine this aspect of your life from a rational and sentimental point of view.

Image Courtesy: Pixabay

Let us assume that you have a home that is 250 square feet. As a tiny home, you can have the entire thing, including the inside of the cabinets and the floors mopped within an hour. What if your house spreads over 2500 ft? If it takes almost an hour to clean 300 square feet (including the floors, cabinets, walls and everything else), then it will take about ten hours to thoroughly clean 2500 square feet. Perhaps you remember as a kid having to clean the house on the weekend, with the help of your family, and you probably used to feel quite lucky if you were able to finish by noon? Well, that sounds about right.

When you have your family to help you, it is quite easy to clean, and it takes less time; however, imagine a situation where you need to do all this cleaning by yourself. It can be quite exhausting in terms of the time and effort that you need to put in to clean about 2500 square feet. You need to spend about ten hours of your time to clean your house.

Not just that, if you have any pets in the family, then you need to clean your house regularly. Imagine if you have a cat or a dog, then you will roughly spend about four to five hours combing out all the stray fur from your furniture and other fixtures in the house. Four hours of cleaning per week amounts to 208 hours of cleaning per year. Woah! That's a lot of time that you need to spend scrubbing and cleaning your house, isn't it?

Now, think of a scenario where you can cut down on the time that you spend cleaning your house. There is a way in which you can do this. You can get rid of the pets, cut down on the clutter and save your time. Well, if you love your pets then you will certainly not get rid of them so the obvious step that you need to take is decluttering. If you can get rid of the clutter from your house, it does become easier to tidy up.

The time that takes to clean your house is directly proportional to the number of things you have in your home. If your house is packed full of things, then you need to clean it regularly. Clutter breeds more clutter. Not just that, you need to constantly reorganize everything to deal with the clutter. Apart from this, if you own your house, then you need to worry about maintenance, upkeep and repairs as well.

We all tend to believe that if we have a large house, then we need to fill it with things. We all tend to look for new things that we can bring home and it eventually reaches a point where you have too much. Decluttering helps you get rid of the items that you will never use, reduce your wardrobe and make some time for the things that matter to you. Once you declutter, you might realize that your home is too big for you. When you adopt the minimalist mindset, it will help you determine how much space you really need.

A person with claustrophobia can live in a house that spreads over 300 square feet and has plenty of windows so you don't really need a big house to be happy. You need a house that is filled with meaningful things, and nothing else, to lead a minimalist life. If you aren't sure that you can live in a small house, then you can test this concept. There are plenty of small homes that are easily available to rent. You can see if you miss any of the clutter, the disoriented way things were accumulated, and the space you have in your home while you live in a small house. You might even find that there are certain things that you can easily live without.

Another way to examine your home, and how much stuff should be there, is whether you can move from that place on an immediate or short notice. For instance, if you have to vacate your home within the next hour, what are all the things that you would grab? You will certainly hold onto those things that are very important to you and you will not worry about the rest. If you feel that there are certain things in your house that you can easily replace, then they aren't all that important to you. It can be quite easy to declutter, minimalize and then organize all that is left over. In your home, you can declutter by getting rid of all the things that you don't need. If you haven't used anything in the last six months, you certainly don't need it anymore. If you aren't certain if you need something or you don't, merely pack them up in boxes and place them in storage. If you can go for about two to three months without missing all the things you boxed up, then it is time to move on.

Digital Life

Image Courtesy: Pixabay

We live in a digital world these days and our digital lives are pretty much exploding. If you want to streamline your personal life, then you need to declutter your digital life. Do you have hundreds of photos that are backed up to the cloud? Do you really need all the files that you stored on the laptop? Do you need multiple computers, laptops or other digital gizmos in your house? Are there things that you can store in digital form and then get rid of their physical forms?

The important question is - what do you do with it all? When you get to the task of decluttering, you need to ask yourself the question and if the answer is not good enough, then you can simply solve it with the help of decluttering. Take a moment and think about the number of times you went to the same place with your camera. How many of those pictures did you upload on any social media site, or did you print? If you don't want to print the pictures or upload them, then why do you need to hold onto them? Do you look at the file you created five years ago about a vacation you took? These are a couple of questions that you can ask if you want to declutter your digital footprint. If you are certain that there are certain physical things that you can convert into digital media, please do so immediately. If you have a bunch of books at home that you want to read, then you can simply find the respective eBook online and you can get rid of the physical copies.

Relationships

Relationships are usually of two types - the people you associate with and the ones you want to include in your life. It can be quite difficult to cut certainties, but that doesn't mean that you cannot reduce your exposure. For the sake of your emotional health, you need to spend time with the ones you love, and limit the time you spend with others. Even if you don't like your family members and aren't too keen on spending too much time with them, you still need to keep them in your life. They are a part of your personal life and you need to understand this.

However, there are certain people you do not have to keep in your life. Friends who cause trouble for you, harm you and do not support you can be readily "decluttered." You do not have to keep toxic relationships alive if they plague you. It is hard, but the answer to the problem exists.

Family - what can you do with them even if you don't want to spend too much time with them? There is one thing that all divorced people learn when they have kids - you can never fully get rid of your spouse, regardless of whether you want them in your life or not. When it comes to family, it is not easy to declutter. There are certain things in your life that you need to put up with because of your family and there is no way around it. It might not seem like a fair situation, but you can certainly minimize such situations. If possible, try to put some distance between the family members you aren't fond of, and yourself.

When it comes to all other relationships that are not family, like your friends, acquaintances or colleagues, then you can decide for yourself. Do you have friends you trust, but they often encourage some behavior that you are trying to change? Your resolve to abstain from doing something tends to become nil. For instance, if you are trying to quit smoking and your friends are habitual smokers who encourage you to smoke, your resolve is bound to dissolve eventually. If your friends mean well for you, then they will support you and will not try to discourage you. If they do, then perhaps you need to reevaluate the company that you keep, or else you can distance yourself. You can decide that until you can say "no," you are not going to be around such friends. If there are any toxic relationships in your life, you need to end those as soon as you can. The way it ends is entirely up to you and the issues that the relationship causes for you. A toxic marriage can end in a divorce, but that doesn't mean that your contact with the spouse ends completely. You can minimalize the way it affects you and you can distance yourself from it. If any relationship in your life doesn't add any value to your life and instead makes you miserable, then please end it.

At the end of the day, you are the only one that's responsible for your happiness.

We all communicate daily; however, learn to communicate your thoughts in a simple and crisp manner and try to end the conversation without indulging in any unnecessary communication. If you prolong unnecessary conversations, it will make you feel quite drained out and will also waste your time. Analyze the communication and conversations you indulge in. If it is important, then spend time on it. If it isn't important, then you need to let go of it.

Emotions

Just like relationships, you need to learn to minimalize your emotions as well. Happy emotions will make you feel good and negative emotions will certainly hamper your productivity. In this section, you will learn about the ways in which you can streamline your emotions and declutter any negative emotions.

Start Setting Reasonable Goals

If you want to declutter your emotional life, then you need to be mentally tough.

You can develop your mental strength by setting reasonable goals for yourself. It is not just about setting goals, but it is about taking the necessary steps to achieve your goals as well. If you want to start working towards your goals, you will need to start applying yourself. It means you will have to ask yourself, 'Am I doing everything I can to fulfill my goals?'. It will not be an easy feat; don't let it scare you. Practice makes a man perfect, and this age-old adage is true! Keep practicing, and you will get better! If you have set some big goals for yourself and they seem impossible, try breaking them down into manageable steps that are doable. For instance, if you want to become assertive, then your first step must be to learn to speak up for yourself at least three times every week. These instances can be major or minor ones However, you need to gauge these events for yourself. Develop a "stick with it" mindset. Even if you face an obstacle or a setback, keep trying and don't give up. Start being resilient and don't worry about the troubles you come across. The goal is to keep going until you achieve what you want to. Think of all the failures as an opportunity to learn, and please do learn from them. Every day is a new day and don't let the troubles from your past sneak up on you.

Don't let Negativity Get a Hold on You

Negativity can sneak up on you quite quickly. It can be stemmed from a negative emotion that you are harboring within yourself or it can be because of something external like negative feedback or toxic people around you. While certain things are beyond your control, the one thing that you can control is the way you feel about yourself and your life. Don't let any negativity live within you. You cannot control what others think about you, but you can certainly control the way you feel about yourself. There are different ways in which you can manage all the negativity. You can start by identifying and challenging such negative thoughts. You can reduce your interaction with harmful and toxic people. If you think you are in a toxic relationship, learn to break free of it. Don't entertain negativity in any form. If a person doesn't contribute to your growth or wellbeing and instead brings you down, stay away from such a person at all costs. At times, you will have to interact with people who are negative, and you cannot avoid such meetings. In such a situation, set some boundaries and don't let their words get to you. Don't take everything personally.

Positive Self-Talk

Make use of positive self-talk for building up your mental strength. Making use of positive affirmations will help you develop a positive outlook while getting rid of all the negativity around you. Take a couple of minutes and look at yourself in the mirror and say something positive and motivating to yourself. You can say something that you believe in, or something that you will like to be true. A couple of positive affirmations that you can make use of are: "I am working on becoming emotionally stronger", "I am learning to manage my stress effectively",

"I'll be kind to myself", and "I am working on achieving my goals, and I will continue to do so", or anything else that you can think of.

Stay Calm, Even Under Pressure

Image Courtesy: Pixabay

Whenever you feel that a particular situation is escalating quickly, and you feel that your emotions are going to boil over, learn to keep your cool. When you learn to control your emotions instead of letting them control you, you are giving yourself an opportunity to weigh in your options before deciding on a particular choice. Take a minute and count to ten before you let a negative emotion boil over. This might sound like a cliché, but it does work. Before having an emotional reaction towards something, take a moment to gather your thoughts and react accordingly. You can try practicing meditation as well, and it can help you maintain your calm. Meditation can help you stay objective while providing you with the necessary time for making sense of your thoughts and emotions. Instead of reacting immediately, you can weigh in your thoughts and emotions and then think of your next step.

Letting Go of Petty Things

If you are always sensitive to the petty annoyances and verbal barbs or taunts that we all tend to come across daily, then you will end up becoming quite bitter. Also, you will be wasting a lot of your precious time and energy thinking about unnecessary things, which don't matter at the end of the day. When you start spending time thinking about all such things and start paying attention to them, you are making them a significant problem that will increase your stress. Learning to adjust your attitude can help you let these petty and trivial issues go without increasing your levels of stress. You are not only preventing the wastage of your valuable time and energy, but you are also saving yourself the trouble of having to deal with extra stress.

Instead of stressing yourself out about all these things, you need to develop a healthy routine of thinking about the things that are bothering you, then take a deep breath, calm yourself down, and, once you are calm, think of the best way in which you can deal with that issue. For instance, if your spouse keeps forgetting to put the cap on the tube of toothpaste after using it, you must understand that such a thing isn't as important to your partner as it is to you. If this bothers you, think about all the other things that your partner does for you that make you feel good and, in comparison, you can certainly let this small flaw of theirs go. Don't try to be a perfectionist, at least not all the time. When you do this, you are setting high expectations for yourself, and these tend to be entirely unrealistic. Try to be realistic while thinking about things and don't let the idea of perfection create any additional stress or burden. You can make use of a straightforward visualization exercise that will help you let go of little things that seem to be bothering you. Take a small stone or pebble and hold it in your hand. Transfer all your negative thoughts that are bothering you into that pebble. Once you are ready, swing it as hard as you can or toss it into a pond. Visualize that all the petty problems are drowning, along with the pebble that's sinking. You are casting away all your negative emotions.

Changing Your Perspective

We tend to get so caught up in the problems that we tend to look at things from a different perspective. A fresh perspective towards existing troubles can help to solve your problems. If you feel like you have hit a dead end with something, take a break and relax. Once you feel refreshed, start thinking of ways in which you can tackle that problem. If you change the way in which you are approaching a problem, you might find a solution to it in no time. Here are a couple of different things that you can try for getting a new perspective on things:

Start reading. Reading the daily news or a book can help you step into someone else's world, and this serves as a good reminder to let you know that the world is a vast place and that your problems are nothing significant when you think about the entirety of the universe we live in. You can start volunteering. When you start interacting with others who can use your help, you certainly will get a different perspective of how things are. Ask your friend for some advice if you feel lost, and make sure that you are thinking about the advice your friend gives you. Step out of your comfort zone and start traveling. It will certainly help you get things in perspective.

Maintaining a Positive Outlook

Image Courtesy: Pixabay

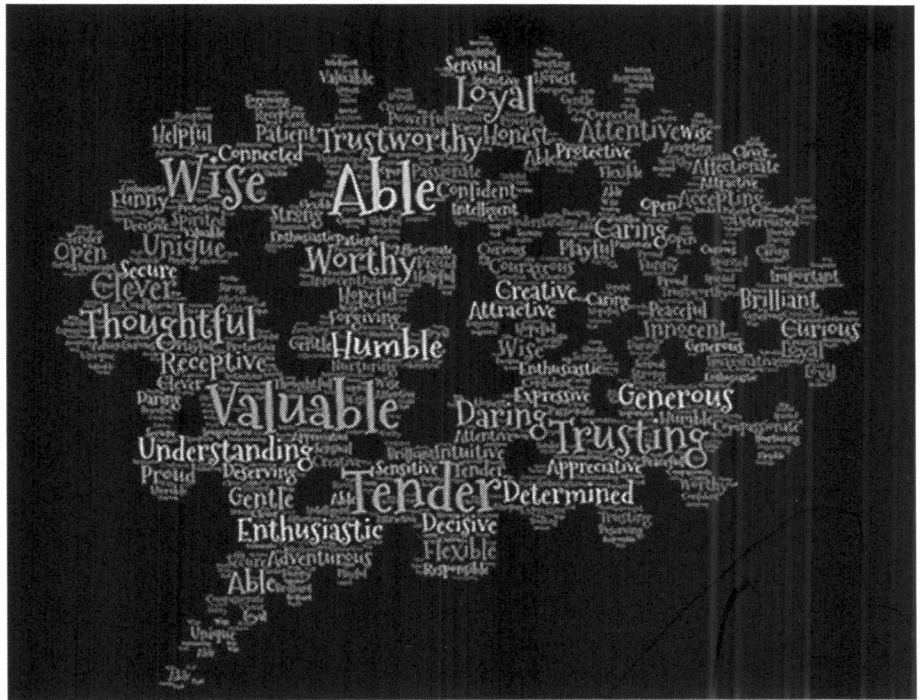

All those who are mentally as well as emotionally strong tend to be happy with what they have. They usually have a positive outlook towards life and don't complain much. This doesn't mean that they don't have any problems. Of course, they have problems just like everyone else, but the difference between them and everyone else is that they can see the bigger picture and know that the challenges they are facing are a part of life. Maintaining a positive outlook towards life will provide you with the mental and the emotional strength that you will need for tackling any problem you come across. Remember that bad times will pass, and the good times are just around the corner. Don't lose hope meantime.

Being Honest with Yourself

The ability to face reality is a sign of your mental and emotional strength. If you are going to overcome a hurdle or a challenge, then you must be able to tackle it head-on. Lying to yourself about your troubles won't make them go away and you will just end up hurting yourself in the process. If you over-eat when you are stressed or sad, accept the fact that there is a problem that needs to be addressed. Don't look for means of escape and try being honest with yourself.

Work Life

Image Courtesy: Pixabay

You need to make sure that you don't carry your personal emotions to your workplace. Try to create a healthy boundary between the two and stick to it as much as you possibly can. Up to a certain point, it is okay to share your problems with your co-workers and listen to theirs; however, it must not be a daily practice and don't encourage it. When you are at work, the only thing that you need to concentrate on is your work and nothing else. If you want to socialize, do so after your working hours. It is difficult to deal with workplace emotions and, ultimately, it can hurt you. You might feel undervalued. You can have issues with a co-worker. Your co-worker probably carries their personal baggage to work and it affects their attitude towards you. Well, don't feel disappointed. There is a simple solution to this problem. You need to keep your personal life private. If you don't open up and share, it will discourage others from doing the same. If you rebuff them because you need to do your work, then they will not stop by.

If you get rid of all the emotional entanglements at work (whether they are feelings of hurt caused because no one seems to recognize your talents, or because of too much personal baggage being brought in), you have the space you need to efficiently work. When you apply the principles of decluttering to your work, then you can easily keep your worries at the door and keep your environment free of all emotions and concentrate only on your work. It is true that there are times when your work life intersects with your personal life. If that's the case, then the only thing that you can do is limit such instances. The power to minimalize all that affects your life is with you, so make use of it.

Make sure that your workspace is neat and tidy. Leave all personal items at home. If you can't, then limit yourself to a photo or two of your loved ones or any other item that motivates you. Before you leave work, you need to tidy up your workspace. Decluttering is an important aspect of keeping the space clean. The way you clean your home, you need to clean your workspace as well. You need to remember that you need to maintain your workspace. A messy workspace will eat at your ability to concentrate. An organized desk helps you focus, while a messy one does the exact opposite.

Make a To-Do List
Making a to-do list is very helpful. Take a sheet of paper and write all the things that you have to complete. You can either do this as soon as you wake up in the morning, or on the previous night. This means that

when you wake up in the morning, you will have a sense of direction, and you will know what needs to be accomplished by the end of the day.

Create a Reward System

Always create a reward system for yourself. Regardless of whether you have completed a small or a big task, you must still reward yourself for completing your work. The reward system doesn't have to be an elaborate one.

Breaking Up Your Workday

Breaks are essential, and you will need a couple of breaks while you are working. It is quite difficult to work efficiently for prolonged periods of time without any breaks. A small break will make you feel fresh, and it will improve your ability to concentrate as well.

Don't Indulge in Any Activities that will Waste Your Time

Image Courtesy: Pixabay

Avoid, or at least try reducing the time you spend indulging in any addictive time-wasting activities. It can be anything, even something as simple as playing a game on your phone can be quite addictive, or constantly checking your social media feed. These activities will not help you accomplish anything, and they just eat into your working hours. Set certain limits. You can do these things while on a break, but not while you are working. Get your work done and then you have plenty of time for all the other activities.

Tackle the Tough Tasks First

There will always be a couple of tasks that you think are tough. It is a good idea to get these tasks out of the way as soon as you possibly can. Don't keep these tasks on hold. Once you are done with these tasks, the rest will be relatively more straightforward.

Discuss Your Goals with Someone

When you tell someone about your goals, you are unknowingly increasing your accountability. It is likely that you will finish a task if you have already told someone about it. You get to decide whom you want to discuss it with. Accountability towards someone else will make you want to complete the task at hand.

If you want to apply the principles of minimalism to your workspace, then you can use the tips mentioned above to improve your productivity.

Life in General

Here are some tips you can follow to improve the way you deal with life in general:

Start Thinking Before Acting

Whenever you feel that you are stuck in a difficult situation, take a while to think things through. Don't react instantly and don't be in a hurry to make a decision. It will provide you with sufficient time for your emotions to diffuse and you can start weighing in your options with an open mind. It is important that you do this, regardless of the situation you are in. If you can afford to, then take some time and list down the pros and cons of a situation. Make a note of how you are feeling as well.

Try finding some positive points about the situation you are in, and this can help change your perspective towards things. At times, the smallest change in perception can make a huge difference. Follow the ten-second rule. Give yourself ten seconds for something to sink in before expressing yourself. Even if your partner tells you that he or she wants to end the relationship, take ten seconds to compose yourself and then respond.

Examining All the Alternatives

Once you have managed to compose yourself, before you decide on the course of action, think clearly about the circumstance you are in. What happened, and what are the possible options available to you? There will always be more than one path that you can opt for. For instance, let us assume that your friend asked you to do something morally wrong and you are torn between your loyalty to your friend and your sense of morality. You will now need to weigh in the different pros and cons and decide accordingly.

Select the Right Path and Stick to It

Make use of your inner voice or your conscience for guiding you. Trust your instincts, and you are likely to be correct. At times, the answer might be quite clear and distinct, but it might be hard to do the right thing. Do not let the problem fester into a more significant hassle than the one it already is. You need to take a call and stick to it. You can always ask others for an opinion and weigh their opinions before concluding, but remember that it needs to be your own decision and no-one else's since you are the one who will have to live with the consequences of it. If you feel like you are stuck, think about what someone you admire would do in such a situation. The decision that you make must be something that you can live with, and don't do something because someone thinks that it is a good idea. Do it because you want to.

Reflect on Your Experiences

Once a problematic situation passes you by, think about the way in which you dealt with it and the outcome of that situation. Will you like to change something about the way you dealt with it, or are you proud of yourself? Remember that wisdom is derived from practice. Examining what happened and the way you dealt with it will help you make any changes the next time you have to deal with a similar situation. If things worked out for you, then it is good; however, if things didn't exactly go as you planned, even that's alright. You had a chance to learn, and that's what it was. It was a learning experience, and you will be careful in future.

Chapter Twelve

Ways to Incorporate Minimalism

Learn to Appreciate

If you cannot appreciate anything in life, then you will never know what is important to you. It helps to highlight and add value to the essential things in your life. When you start to appreciate, you will realize that there are plenty of things to appreciate. When you wake up in the morning, did you ever feel appreciative of anything? You can be thankful for something as simple as your bed, your friends, your family, or even your job. Make it a habit that, while waking up and while going to sleep, you must remind yourself of three things in your life that you are appreciative of.

Morning Routine

Image Coutesy: Pixabay

Morning helps to set the tone for the rest of the day. If you have a well-established morning routine, then you will feel entirely focused, energized, and positive about the rest of the day. You can do yoga, exercise, meditate, watch some inspirational videos, or read anything that's motivational. You need to set yourself up for a good day if you want it to be good.

Practice Acceptance

More often than not, things don't necessarily go as planned. You might feel frustrated when your plans change, or when they don't work in your favor; however, resistance doesn't change anything, and things just go downhill from there. When you start accepting what has happened, only then can you let go of all the unnecessary suffering. You need to practice acceptance, understand and adjust yourself to a circumstance, without any conflicting emotions clouding your judgment.

Living in the Present

You must live in the present, because that's where everything happens, and it is the only place where you can experience happiness. Your past might be full of beautiful memories, but you cannot get anything from those memories. By living in the past or the future, you forget about the moment that you have in hand. Your present is critical, and you need to start living in it as well. Gadgets happen to be a significant part of our lives these days, and social media is an even more substantial part. Your online presence needs to go hand in hand with your offline life as well. Learn to live in the present, physically. It isn't about living in the virtual world all the time; it doesn't make any sense.

Listening Attentively

Image Courtesy: Pixabay

Listening and hearing are two different concepts altogether, even though these words are used interchangeably. Listening is a conscious process where you need to pay attention. It helps to establish a strong bond between people and assists you to live in the present; therefore, it is an excellent source of happiness. You need to make a conscious effort to be more present while having a conversation with anyone.

Materialistic Things Don't Matter

Money can help you buy things, and worldly things will assist in making you feel momentarily satisfied. Why don't you try saving up for 6 months without shopping unnecessarily? You will be able to save a small fortune, and you can make use of that money to travel instead. Instead of filling your life with all sorts of expensive branded products, you need to try to create beautiful memories that will make you feel happy whenever you think about them.

Always Dream Big

Dreams provide you with the motivation to keep going, so always try to dream big. Your dream will assist you in finding the one thing that you are passionate about. Let yourself dream and have sufficient faith in your ability to turn that dream into reality. You can always spend 5 minutes daily and step into your dream world. Start visualizing the things that you want to do and how amazing you will feel once you achieve your dreams. Try making your visualization as real as possible, and it will increase your desire to work towards that goal.

Take Steps towards Your Dreams

Does your present look anything like the future that you have been dreaming about? If not, spend some time and energy thinking about the various things that you can do for ensuring your growth. You don't have to do everything at once. Start by taking small steps, and you will ultimately reach your goal.

Change Your Mindset

The way you experience the world depends entirely on your perception of it. When you feel that there is a scarcity, you will start hoarding; however, when you start letting go of things, it just signifies that you have more than enough. If you feel unloved, why don't you try giving showing love to someone else who needs it? Change your mindset, and things will follow.

Give Yourself a Break

The society that we live in has made us believe that we need to keep doing as much as we possibly can without any time to recharge. Neither your mind nor your body is an infallible machine and treating it like one will not do you any good. It is essential that you give yourself some time to reenergize yourself. Take a couple of short breaks and maybe a power nap or two. It is necessary to understand that your body cannot function without rest, and a break will help revitalize your body and mind. Not many of us take into consideration the need for breaks so, while planning for something, consider the downtime.

Time to Play

Don't think of living as a duty that you have been entrusted with. You don't have to complete the to-do list, or even try fixing everything that is broken. You need to start thinking about how amazing it is that you are alive, and that life can be quite magical. Take a couple of minutes every day and do something just because it is fun. It can be something as silly as jumping on the trampoline. If it makes you feel like a child again, give it a try.

Surround Yourself with Happy People

Image Courtesy: Pixabay

Attitude can be quite contagious. If you are surrounded by people who are smiling, then it is quite likely that you will start laughing as well. If someone was unpleasant to you, you'd probably be rude too. Surround yourself with people who are happy. Try limiting negativity and negative people from your life as much as you possibly can.

Moving Slowly

We are always in a rush to get from one place to the other. In our haste, we forget to appreciate a lot. Faster doesn't always mean better and busy doesn't mean growth, so slow down. Put all your energy and focus on the things that you are doing.

Soothing Yourself Actively

The only thing that matters is the manner in which you deal with the things that happen in your life. If you want to be able to make better decisions, then you need to start soothing your negative thoughts. Whenever you feel wrong about something, try rationalizing it. Alternatively, you can go for a run, meditate, or make a note of things that you love about your life.

Learn to Let Go

Letting go might not be easy, but it is the only way in which you can open yourself up to better things in life. If you keep holding on to all your baggage, you will not have any space left to welcome new things into your life. When you let go, your mind will feel at ease. It helps to let new perspectives take birth. Start by actively practicing letting go of things that don't do you any good, like complaining, unnecessary comparisons, negativity, your past mistakes, or future worries.

Forgiveness

Forgive and forget. It doesn't make any sense if you keep holding onto something that someone said or did a while ago. Forgiveness helps you move forward, and holding onto unnecessary memories or emotions will not do you any good whatsoever. Learn to forgive others. Maybe they did you some wrong, but, be the bigger person and let go. It is not just about forgiving others, but you must learn to forgive yourself as well.

Start Taking Care of Yourself

Your body, mind, and soul are interconnected. A change in any of them results in a change in all three. Do something to improve your overall wellbeing. You must start taking care of yourself.

Start Strong

You must start your day with a bang. As soon as you wake up, do something that will make the rest of the day a success for you. It is the trick that you need to get right. It is quite easy to roll out of bed, check your email, or watch some TV. It will just make your day meaningless. Doesn't it feel good when you have made some progress on something that's meaningful in your life? Then why don't you do something about it? The previous night, before sleeping, make a simple plan as to the first task that you need to tackle in the morning. It can be something as simple as working out for an hour. What is that one thing that will make your day a success? It can be anything. If you know what it is, then get to it the minute you wake up in the morning.

Plan Less

You don't have to rush through your day. Rushing through things will not only stress you out, but it will also kill your happiness. Stop believing that you don't have the time to enjoy the things around you. Take some time and smell the roses. There is always time and don't be under the misconception that you need to hurry up all the time. If you don't take some time out, the roses will die eventually. Plan to do maybe one or two critical things daily. Don't fill up your entire calendar with tasks that you need to accomplish. Human beings tend to have ridiculous notions about what they can achieve, and how quickly they can get things done. All this just adds to the stress and disappointment you might feel, so stop planning every moment of your day.

Getting Lost in Happiness

Take a few minutes and think about all those bits of your life that you are grateful for. It can be something big or small. Things that you are proud of, the things that make you smile, and the things you enjoy; the people who mean a lot to you, and those whom you are grateful to have around yourself. You can do this anywhere you are. You can do this while at work, while working out, or even while traveling. When you start feeling sheer gratitude, it is not possible to handle any form of negative emotions like stress or anger.

Knowing the Reason

We all must have things that make us instantly happy. The things that make you smile inspire you, or just make you happy. It can be a movie, a song, a video, a specific book, or even a friend. Make sure that you keep track of these things. Spend a few minutes and make this list. Keep adding to things whenever you notice that something puts a smile on your face. The next time you are feeling low, just refer to this list.

Always Smile

It is the simplest and the most powerful thing you can do. It is as contagious as it gets. Keep smiling. Strive to be known as the person who is always smiling. If you see someone frowning, smile at them. Smile the biggest smile you possibly can. All it takes is a few people to reciprocate the same, and, after this, it will just keep on spreading. Also, studies show that smiling creates a chemical reaction in the brain that makes us happy.

Be Around those Who Make You Happy

When you are feeling low, the last thing you will want to do is be around other people. Resist doing this at any cost. Life is about forming relationships and connections. The ones you love can change your mood in an instant. Make sure that you choose people carefully. You need people who are positive and who will bring positivity into your life.

Anyone who doesn't fit this bill is probably not worth your while. Stay away from negative people and all forms of negativity.

Selfless

Being selfless can make you happy too. Do something good for someone else. It is bound to make you feel better about yourself. It can be something as simple as just holding the door open for someone, or letting someone else get ahead of you in the queue. It doesn't have to be anything extravagant. The smallest of deeds can make you feel happy.

There are some days when you feel like there's rocket fuel pumping through your body, and days when you feel like you can overcome anything that life throws at you, but there are those days when it feels like everything is weighing down on you. Have you ever felt like this? Well, haven't we all? If you want to incorporate minimalism into your daily life, then you need to work on it consciously. It is not just a practice, but also a daily choice.

Chapter Thirteen

Ideas to Simplify Your Life

A simple life tends to mean different things and a different value for every individual. For instance, for some, it can mean to eliminate all things but the necessities, strive for chaos over peace and perhaps spend time doing things that are meaningful to you. It can mean one or all of these things and much more. It means to get rid of certain things that you do to make time for things and people that you love. It can mean to get rid of clutter so that all you are left with are the things that lend value to your life, but it isn't always a simple process to get to simplicity. Often, it can seem like two steps forward and one step back. There is no step-by-step guide to simplify your life. You can start with any aspect of your life and then move on to the next one. If you want to simplify your life, then go through the list that's given in this section.

List the Top Four or Five Things

You need to make a list of the top four or five important things. What means the most to you? What do you value the most? What are the four or five things that you want to do the most in your life? To simplify your life, you need to prioritize. If you cannot prioritize, then you will never know what is important to you and what isn't. If you want to make room for important things in life, then the first step is to identify those things.

Evaluate

You need to evaluate all your commitments. Take a look at all the things that you are doing in your life. It means you need to evaluate everything from the work that you do in your personal and professional life. Think about all those things that add value to your life and the things that you enjoy. Which of these things are in sync with your priorities? You need to immediately let go of all those things that don't seem like a priority.

Time

What does a typical day in your life look like? How do you spend the 24-hours available to you in a day? What are all the things that you do, from the moment you wake up in the morning until you go to bed at night? Make a list of all these things and then see whether they are in sync with your priorities or not. If not, then you simply need to eliminate those things and focus on what is important. You need to redesign your day.

Work Tasks

A typical workday consists of an endless list of tasks that you need to work on. At least, that seems to be the case with most people these days. If your aim is to simply strike off the tasks on your to-do list, then you will not be able to get much work done and will not get to the important stuff. You need to focus on the essential tasks and the rest can wait.

Home Tasks

Along the same line of thought, you need to look at all the things that you do at home. At times, the list of home tasks can be as long as the work list. If you don't prioritize, at the end of the day you might have spent all your time on things that mean little to you.

Say No

If you want to simplify your life, you need to learn to say no. You need to be able to say no to yourself as well as those around you. It will save you unnecessary work and trouble. If you cannot say no, you will often find yourself in such situations wherein you will feel like you have certainly bitten off more than you can chew.

Communication

There are various means of communication these days and the means just seem to be increasing by the day, so it doesn't come as a surprise that our lives are filled with multiple flows of communication. Communication can be in the form of email, cell phones, paper mail, Skype, Twitter and various other platforms. If you let it, then all this can take up your valuable time and you will not even realize it. Itis important that you restrict the time that you spend on this. Make sure that you check your mail only at certain times of the day, and restrict your phone calls to a certain number of minutes and so on. You need to set a schedule and make sure that you stick to it as well.

Media Usage

This tip might not appeal to a lot of people. Do you realize the amount of time you spend watching TV, surfing the net or the like? Well, if you don't, then take a moment to think about it. Most of us tend to while away our time on this. Media is an important part of our lives these days, but you need to understand that there's more to life than binge-watching shows on Netflix. You can simplify your life and concentrate on other important things if you reduce the time you spend on this.

Purge

You need to purge yourself of all the things that you own. Set a weekend aside for this and work on purging the things that you don't need. Gather a couple of boxes and trash bags for all the things that you want to donate or toss respectively.

Big Items

We all tend to clutter our lives with things over a period of time. You probably don't even realize when you start to gather clutter. The first thing that you need to do is get rid of all the big items that you no longer use. For instance, do you have a television in your house that doesn't work, or a dishwasher that you don't use? Well, it is a good idea to get rid of this and make space for something significant.

Simplicity Statement

What do you think your simple life will look like? What do you think minimalism means to you? How does it translate into your life? Take a couple of moments and think about all this and write it down. Make a simple statement and keep reading it daily.

Free Up Some Time

Think of ways in which you can free up a little time for the important things in your life. It means that you need to eliminate doing all the things that you don't like, cut back on those things that waste your time and, instead, you need to make some room for the things that you want to do.

Do What You Love

Image Courtesy: Pixabay

Once you free up a little time, make sure that you spend this time to do the things that you like. It can be something as simple as spending time with your spouse, children and friends, or it can be something else that you are passionate about. Refer to the first tip and go through the 4-5 things that are your priorities. All the free time that's available to you, you can now spend on things that you enjoy.

People You Love

The list of 4-5 important things that you made probably includes some people you love. If it doesn't, then perhaps you need to reconsider the list. The people you love can include your spouse, children, partner, parents, close friends, family members or anyone else. Take some time out of your schedule and spend this time with your loved ones.

Alone Time

You don't have to surround yourself with people all the time. You need to take some time out of your daily routine for yourself as well. Spend some time by yourself and learn to be comfortable with yourself. You can meditate for a while daily, or create a relaxing bath routine for yourself. Get used to the quiet and give your inner voice a chance to come through.

Image Courtesy: Pixabay

Eat Slowly

Don't just stuff yourself up with food whenever you eat. Learn to savor the taste of the food you eat. Enjoy the different flavors and textures. Once you become conscious of all that you eat, you will slowly start to eat healthy food as well. Chew your food thoroughly before you swallow it. Make sure that you have your meals at the dining table and don't watch any television or spend your time on any gadgets.

Drive Slowly

Well, who likes being stuck in traffic? No-one does. If you honk, get angry, feel frustrated or stressed out whenever you are stuck in traffic, take a moment and think about it. Does all this help you navigate the traffic? No, it doesn't. In fact, all it does is endanger you and those around you. Instead, you need to drive slowly and safely. It can be quite peaceful when you drive slowly. Don't let all this unnecessary frustration and irritation clutter your mind with negativity.

Be Present

You need to learn to be present in the moment. The simple phrase "be present" can make all the difference when you try to simplify your life. You need to live in the moment. How many of us live in the moment? Most of us tend to think about the past or worry about the future all the time. When you do this, you tend to let go of the present. When you live in the present, you will become aware of your life and of all the things that are going on around you. Take some time out of your hectic life and slow down. Enjoy all the things that are happening around you.

Streamline

Most of us tend to live our lives in an unplanned manner. We have various complex systems in place because most of us don't give it any conscious thought. Instead, you need to learn to focus on one thing at a time. Whenever you decide to focus on one thing, make sure that it is the only thing that you are concentrating on and nothing else. Create a simplified and efficient system to go through life. If you don't streamline your life, it will not make any sense and you will quickly lose your way in the grand scheme of things.

Clean Your Desk

It is important that you organize your workspace. A cluttered desk can be quite distracting, and it can even be stressful. If you have a clean desk, you can work better, and it improves your ability to think. Not just that, an organized workspace improves your efficiency as well. Just keep the bare essentials on the desk and remove everything else.

Routine

If you want to simplify your life, then you need to create some routines for yourself. You can create a morning routine, an evening routine, or a bill-paying routine and so on. You can create a routine for pretty much anything in your life.

Consolidate Email Accounts

You can create an email account for free and most people tend to have at least two email addresses. You need to consolidate all your email accounts and you can do this by setting up redirecting rules or by forwarding the messages to your primary email. If you do this, then you don't have to constantly check different email accounts throughout the day. Instead, you need to just check your primary email account.

You can also use disposable email accounts. Most of us tend to receive a lot of spam mails and other unnecessary promotional content. You can use a throwaway email account for all unnecessary mails and direct all the important mails only to the primary email account. If you do this, you can successfully reduce the spam and the junk mail you receive.

Image Courtesy: Pixabay

Automate Your Finances

There might be certain recurring bills that you need to pay monthly like your phone bill, water or electricity bill, maintenance, EMI on loan and so on. Well, you can simplify the process of payment of these bills by setting your finances on autopilot. You can link the payments of certain bills to a particular bank account and the bills will be automatically deducted from the account as and when they are due. If you do this, then you don't have to worry about writing checks or depositing payments.

Expensive Subscriptions

Take a look at your monthly bills and see if there are any subscriptions or memberships that you don't use. If you don't use a particular membership, then it is better to cancel it. For instance, does anyone really need Hulu, Prime and Netflix subscriptions at the same time? Similarly, you can cancel any unused subscriptions or bills. It might just seem like a couple of dollars, but it can all add up to a significant amount. For instance, the monthly Netflix subscription fee is almost $11 and if you don't use this subscription, then you can save up to $132 annually!

Junk Mail

You need to clean your inbox regularly. Do you feel that your email is overflowing with new emails as well as messages? Do these messages just seem to keep piling up? If so, then there is nothing abnormal about it. Make it a point to check your mail, save the important ones and then delete the rest. All those emails and messages that aren't important or useful, you can delete them.

Live Frugally

If you want to live a minimalist lifestyle, then you need to learn a little frugally. It means that you need to want less, buy less and leave less of a footprint on the earth. It is directly proportional to your idea of simplicity. It doesn't mean that you cannot enjoy the finer things in life. It simply means that you must not spend on things that you don't need. Keep your wants in check and buy things only when you need them.

Minimalist Home

A minimalist home is free of clutter and there isn't much in it apart from the things that are necessary. Not just that, a house that is free of clutter is quite peaceful as well.

A Small Home

If you can get rid of all the unnecessary things in your life, then you will realize that you probably don't need all the space that you have. You don't have to live on a boat (unless you are happy doing so), but you can certainly live a comfortable life in a smaller home. It will be less expensive than a bigger home. A smaller house is easier to maintain and will help you live a simple life.

Small Car

It is certainly a big move; however, if you have a big car or an SUV, you might not really need anything this big. It is more expensive, uses a lot of gas, it is hard to maintain and not to mention the fact that it takes a lot of parking space. You can simplify your life with a smaller car. You don't need to opt for the tiniest car available, and you don't have to act on it immediately. You can take some time and think about it from a long-term perspective.

Enough

The materialistic society that we live in is all about getting more and more. There doesn't seem to be an end to the number of things that you can obtain. Sure, you can purchase the latest gadgets, clothes, shoes and other things; however, when will you be able to know when enough is enough? Most people don't realize this and tend to keep buying more than what they need. It is a vicious cycle that doesn't end. Break free of this cycle and figure out what "enough" means to you.

Weekly Dinner Menu

It can be quite stressful and not to mention a little annoying when you need to figure out what you need to eat for dinner daily. Most people don't realize it, but we tend to spend a lot of time thinking about what to eat. If you have a pre-decided menu, then you can save yourself a lot of hassle. Not just that, when you plan your meals in advance, you can buy the groceries accordingly and plan for healthy meals.

Eat Healthily

What does eating healthily have to do with simplicity? These two topics don't seem to be related, do they? Well, take a moment and think about it. If you eat unhealthy food all the time, it will deteriorate your health and cause several health problems and complications in the long run. Maybe not immediately, but a couple of years down the line your unhealthy eating habits can lead to a steady decline in health. All this

151

translates into hefty medical bills. You get the idea, don't you? Being unhealthy is quite complicated. If you can eat healthy meals, you can avoid all the unnecessary medical bills in the future.

Exercise

It goes along the same lines as eating healthy. It helps simplify your life in the long run, and the benefits that exercise offers don't end at that. Exercising regularly not only acts as a stress buster, but elevates your mood as well. If you want to feel good about yourself, de-stress, or if you want to lead a healthy life, then you need to exercise regularly.

Declutter Before You Organize

You cannot organize the things in your life if you don't declutter. Only when you declutter will you be able to realize what are the important and not so important things in your life. It doesn't make any sense to try and organize an overstuffed closet without decluttering. When you declutter your wardrobe or closet, then you can organize all the things in it. Decluttering before organizing also makes it simple to organize.

Inner Simplicity

Do you think you are a spiritual person? Well, you don't necessarily have to be a spiritual person to try this tip. Spend some time with yourself and, after a while, you will realize that it gives you some inner peace and takes away a little of the chaos that you feel. You can spend some time meditating, praying, journaling your feelings or by doing anything that will make you feel at peace. Working on your inner peace is a good idea.

Decompress

The hectic lives that we lead these days are filled with stress. Regardless of how much you simplify your life, stress isn't something that you can ever escape. Stress seems to be a constant part of our lives these days and, therefore, it is quintessential that you learn to decompress from the stress that you experience. Take a couple of minutes out of your daily schedule to indulge in any activity that will reduce the stress that you experience. It can be something as simple as reading a book, spending time with your pet, taking a walk or even talking to someone you love.

Car

A car is one of the essential things that you will need to live a comfortable life, but do you think you can live without your car? Okay, if the thought of not having a car scares you, then perhaps you can think about reducing its usage. You can considerably reduce your expenses if you cut down on the usage of a car. You don't have to worry about the insurance bills, the gas bills or any other expenses related to maintenance if you don't have a car.

Self-Expression

Find a creative outlet to express yourself. You can try your hand at writing, painting, drawing, singing, poetry, creating movies, dancing or anything else. If you want more from life, then you need to know about yourself and understand yourself.

Goals

Instead of having a dozen goals or even more, you need to simplify it all. Simplify it to one major goal and work on achieving it. Not only will this be less stressful, but it will increase your rate of success as well. It will give you a better chance to be successful. It is fine even if you cannot simplify all of your goals. You need to make it a point to work on one goal before you move onto the next one. If you try working on too many things at once, it is quite likely that you will not be able to do much good and cannot justify your goals.

Multitasking

The rule that applies to your goals applies to your ability to multitask as well. Don't try to do more than one thing at a time. Work on one thing, and complete it before you move on to the next one. If you try to work on multiple things at once, you will not be able to concentrate on anything and everything will merely seem like a mess. Most people seem to think that multitasking saves them time. It might seem like that, but that's certainly not the case.

The one question that you need to ask yourself constantly when you try to simplify your life is "Will this simplify my life?" If the answer is yes, then go ahead and get on with it, but, if the answer is no, then you need to reevaluate the task at hand.

For all those cynics who feel that the list mentioned above is quite long, then there are two simple steps that you can take to simplify your life. The first step is to identify all that's important to you, and the second step is to get rid of everything else.

Conclusion

I want to thank you once again for choosing this book, and I hope it proved to be an enjoyable read.

You have gone from gaining knowledge about minimalism and a minimalist mindset to transitioning into it, with an eye towards decluttering as your first step to become a minimalist. You are well on your way to a happier and a clutter-free life. There are a couple of steps that you need to work on. Even though you have already begun your new habits, you have to face the setbacks and learn how to work through them.

It is not easy to develop a new habit, and it certainly is not easy to let go of an old habit. Well, if you are worried that, while trying to adopt a minimalist lifestyle you might revert to your old habits, you can put all those worries to rest. Whenever you feel like you are deviating from minimalism, or feel that your old habits are creeping back in, you merely need to go through this book. If you feel like you are struggling with a particular aspect of minimalism, then re-read the section you struggled with and try again. You might need to go a little slower, you may need to speed up, or you might need to declutter a bit more than you have.

The journey is not easy. Emotions play a big role in what you are attempting. Do not lose hope. Find a support team and talk about your journey into the minimalist mindset as others have done.

The reward is what you set, but the one thing that is always true - is that you are going to be happier, less stressed and have more time to do the things you love. Hard work is necessary. No-one ever got anything in life for free that didn't have to pay up later. Eventually, the piper would call, whether it was for the money to pay the debt gained, or a favor for all the favors you received.

Minimalism can help you turn your life around. Once you start to prioritize things in your life, you will be able to concentrate on the things that do matter and let go of everything else. The key to a happy life is to do things that make you happy and spend time with people who make you happy. Minimalism and decluttering will help you with these objectives so it is safe to say that the key to your happiness rests in your hands. Now that you know what minimalism is about, it is time for you to take the first step to turn your life around.

Finally, if you found this book useful in anyway, a review on Amazon is always appreciated. Thank you, and all the best!

Sources

https://zenhabits.net/simple-living-manifesto-72-ideas-to-simplify-your-life/

https://www.theminimalists.com/radical/

https://www.apartmenttherapy.com/these-are-the-6-types-of-minimalists-which-one-are-you-250532

https://www.therusticelk.com/32-tips-on-becoming-a-minimalist/

https://www.apartmenttherapy.com/seeking-simplicity-how-to-start-living-a-more-minimal-lifestyle-210936

http://www.simplyfiercely.com/minimalism-goal-setting/

http://www.markmerrill.com/7-ways-to-know-whats-truly-important-to-you/

https://zenhabits.net/the-first-rule-of-simplifying-identify-the-essential-or-how-to-avoid-the-void/

https://clutterfreenow.com/blog/decluttering/decluttering-for-beginners-5-rules-to-encourage-you-to-let-go/

https://www.elitedaily.com/life/things-need-stop-immediately-want-live-stress-free-life/659777

http://www.beigerenegade.com/2016/02/25/seven-principles-for-decluttering-your-life/

https://makespace.com/blog/posts/minimalist-living-tips/

https://theartofsimple.net/declutteringtruths/

Printed in Great Britain
by Amazon